Editorial Project Manager
Mara Ellen Guckian

Managing Editors
Karen Goldfluss, M.S. Ed.
Ina Massler Levin, M. A.

Art Coordinator
Renée Christine Yates

Cover Artist
Barb Lorseyedi

Art Production Manager
Kevin Barnes

Imaging
James Edward Grace

Publisher
Mary D. Smith, M.S. Ed.

Author

Tracy Edmunds, M.S. Ed.

Teacher Created Resources, Inc.
6421 Industry Way
Westminster, CA 92683
www.teachercreated.com
ISBN-1-4206-3183-7

Teacher Created Resources

Table of Contents

Graph Cutouts

Introduction

Year Round Charts and Graphs is a full-color collection of resources for teaching graphing in Pre-K and kindergarten classrooms.

Why Teach Graphing?

Young children are just beginning to grasp abstract concepts such as letters and numbers. Using graphs in the classroom can help students understand that concrete objects and ideas can be represented in different ways. Graphs and charts are also ideal tools for providing children with opportunities to use their developing number sense and problem-solving skills every day.

How to Use This Book

The first part of this book includes blank graph forms that you can assemble and use in your classroom, along with instructions and ideas for using these forms effectively.

First, read through *Introducing Graphing* to your students (pages 4–6). Next, pull out and assemble the large bar graph (instructions, page 8; graph, pages 9–24) and begin graphing with your students. Ideas for graphing topics can be found on page 56 and at the beginning of each cutout section.

Once your students have some experience with bar graphs, move on to Venn diagrams (pages 37–42), pie charts (pages 43–48), and line graphs (pages 49–53). Each section includes instructions for using the graphs with your students.

The second part of this book provides full-color cutouts that you and your students can use to create many different charts and graphs throughout the school year. The first page of each section gives you label cards and ideas for graph topics using these cutouts. Suggestions for other topic-related graphs are included. For instance, if you are graphing who has been to a farm and who has not, you might have students place a dot sticker, sticky note, or their portrait cards in the *Yes* or the *No* column of a bar graph or chart to indicate their responses. These are the 10 units:

Farm Animals

Sea Animals

Creepy Crawlies

Dinosaurs

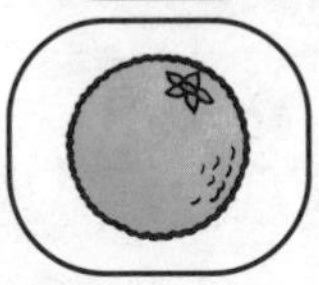
Fruit

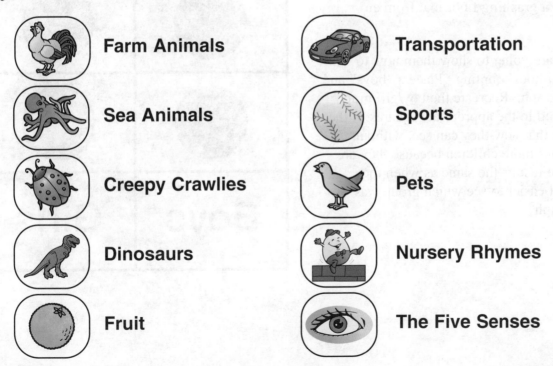

Transportation

Sports

Pets

Nursery Rhymes

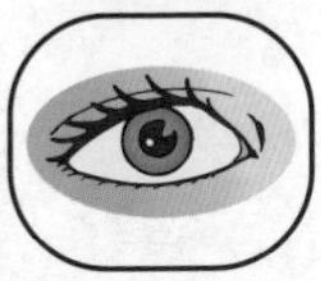
The Five Senses

Introducing Graphing

Young children are just beginning to learn that concrete objects can be represented in different ways. For example, a dog is a furry animal that wags its tail and barks. It can be represented by a photograph of a dog, a stylized or "cartoon" illustration of a dog, or letters forming the word "dog." Graphs and charts can help students make this critical transition from concrete to representative.

Introducing Concrete Graphs

Gather your students and tell them that the class is going to work together to find out if there are more boys or girls in the class. Ask them to form a boys' line and a girls' line. Then, compare the two lines to try to answer the question. Point out to students that their lines can get longer or shorter based on how close they stand to each other—you can have them demonstrate by spreading out and then moving closer together. Ask them how they can tell which line has more children. Students will probably say that they should count the children in line, so count and discuss the results. Tell students that later you will show them a different way to answer the question.

Create a large bar graph on the floor of your classroom using painter's tape (available at home centers and paint stores — it's easy to remove) or masking tape, making each square large enough for a child to stand in. You could also use tape to create a graph on a large vinyl tablecloth or purchase a graphing floor mat from an educational supplier.

Tell students that you are going to show them how to tell which line is longer without counting. Place a "boys" and a "girls" label on the graph. Recreate the boy/girl graph by having students stand in the appropriate squares of the floor graph. Point out that now they can see, without counting, which line has more children because they are spaced evenly. Are the results the same as when they stood in a line? Was it easier to see which group was larger by using the graph?

Introducing Graphing *(cont.)*

Use many different "real" items to give students varied experiences with graphing. Your floor graph can be used vertically (columns) or horizontally (rows). (*Note:* You may need to expand your floor graph from two columns to three, four, or even five rows/columns.) Label the columns or rows of your graph. Index cards, word or sentence strips, or sheets of paper work well—just print the label for each column/row in large letters and place it on the floor in the appropriate space. Try the following ideas to get started:

- Have each student remove one shoe and place it in the floor graph according to the color of the shoe or the type of fastening (laces, Velcro, buckles, etc.).
- Graph the class' favorite colors by asking each student to bring a small item from home in his or her favorite color for the floor graph.
- Give students name cards and have them place their cards in the floor graph according to the number of letters in their names.

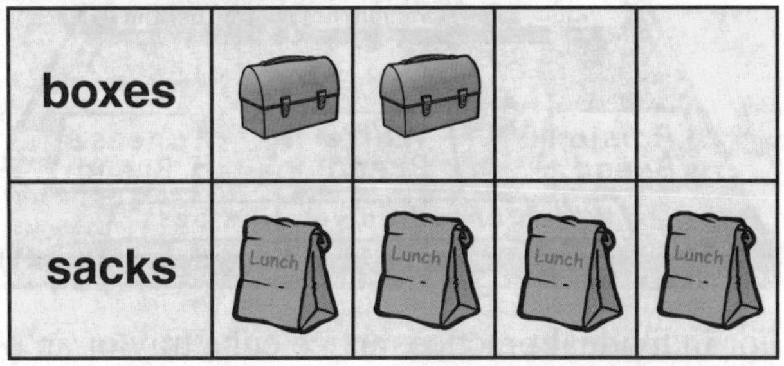

- Let students place their snacks in the floor graph to see how many lunchboxes and how many paper sacks are being used.

Moving On to Representative Graphs

When students are comfortable using the floor graph, work on transitioning from graphs with concrete objects to representations of those objects. Before students come into class, use the bar graph forms on pages 9 to 23 to create a large bar graph and display it on the wall. (See page 8 for instructions.) Label one column "girls" and a second column "boys." Use the number cards (pages 25–28) to label the graph. Additional columns may be left blank.

Make copies of the Portrait Cards on page 7, cut them out, and give one to each student. Let students create self-portraits by coloring and drawing on the cards to show their eye and skin colors and to add their hair. If appropriate, students can add their names to the bottom of their pictures. Alternatively, give each student a photograph of himself or herself with double-sided or looped tape on the back. (Be sure the photographs will fit in the 2 ½" [6 cm] squares on the graph.) If you laminate these self-portraits, you can use them throughout the school year.

Have students re-create their boy/girl concrete graph by standing on the taped floor graph, holding their self-portraits. Then, have each student come up and stick his or her self-portrait on the pictograph hanging on the wall. Ask students to compare the pictograph to their floor graph. Are the results the same? Discuss how the bar graph on the wall tells the same story as the bar graph on the floor, but uses less space.

Introducing Graphing *(cont.)*

Moving On to Representative Graphs *(cont.)*

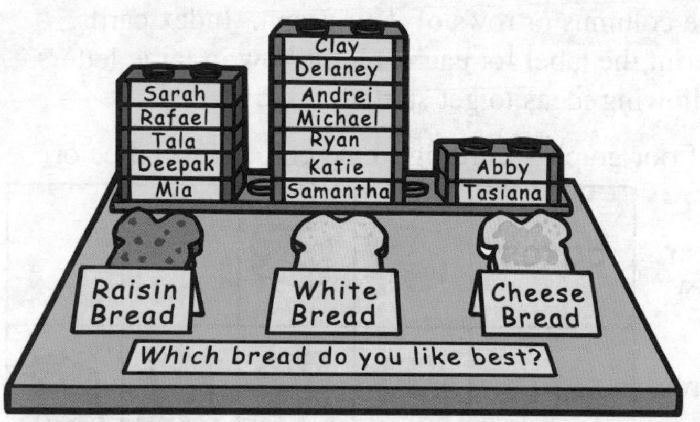

Continue to provide opportunities for students to turn concrete floor graphs into representative graphs. For example, select two or three books that your students are familiar with. Have students "vote" for their favorite by standing in the floor graph in the appropriate column. Give each student a block with a name card taped on it and ask them to "vote" for their favorite by stacking their block next to the actual book.

For individual practice, an ice cube tray or an egg carton can make a great graph, used either horizontally or vertically. For example, give each student a small handful of counters in two colors. Have them sort the counters into two groups by color, then place one counter in each section of the egg carton or ice cube tray, one color in one column/row, and the other color in the other column/row. Next, provide a copy of the individual 2-column or 2-row bar graph (The vertical graph is on page 29 and the horizontal graph is on page 30.) and have the students transfer the counters to the graph. Then, show the students how to color in the square under each counter with the matching color. Help students label their graphs. Follow up by asking some of the Graph Analysis questions on page 55. Lists of items that can be graphed can be found on page 56.

Individual students can choose their own graphing questions, such as, "Can you skip?" or "What is your favorite flavor of ice cream?" Let students take a survey by having classmates or family members sign their names or make tally marks under their choices, then show students how to transfer their data to a bar graph (pages 8–36).

Once students are comfortable with bar graphs, you can move on to Venn diagrams, pie charts, and line graphs.

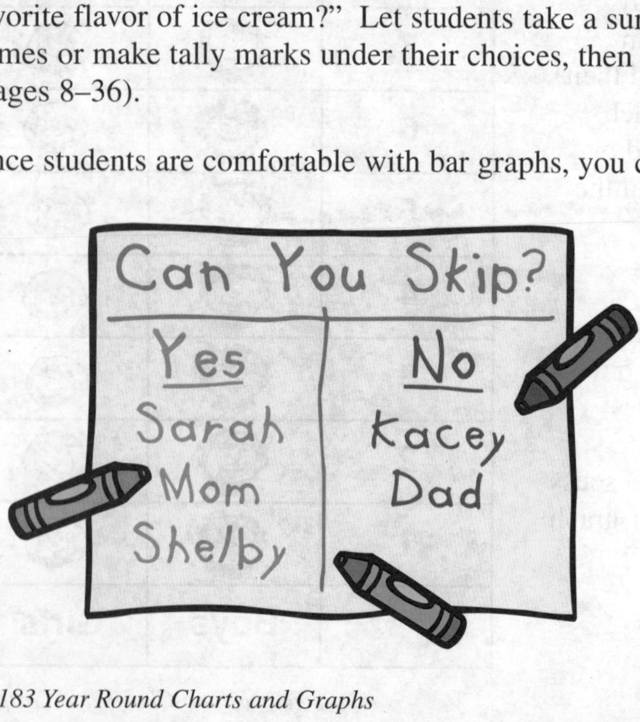

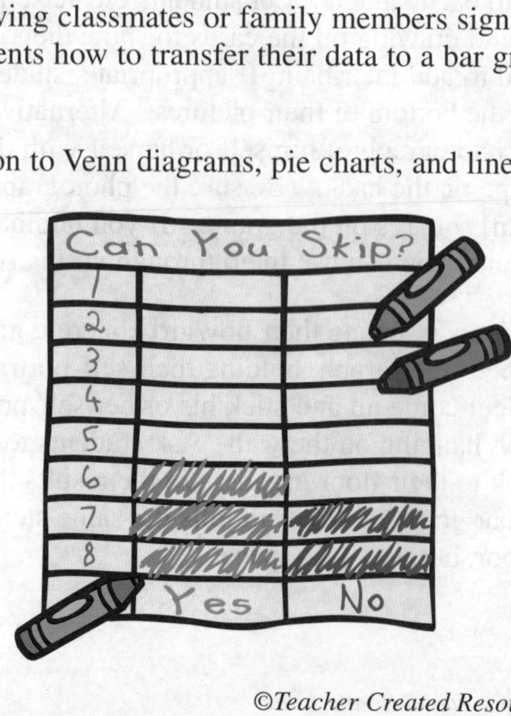

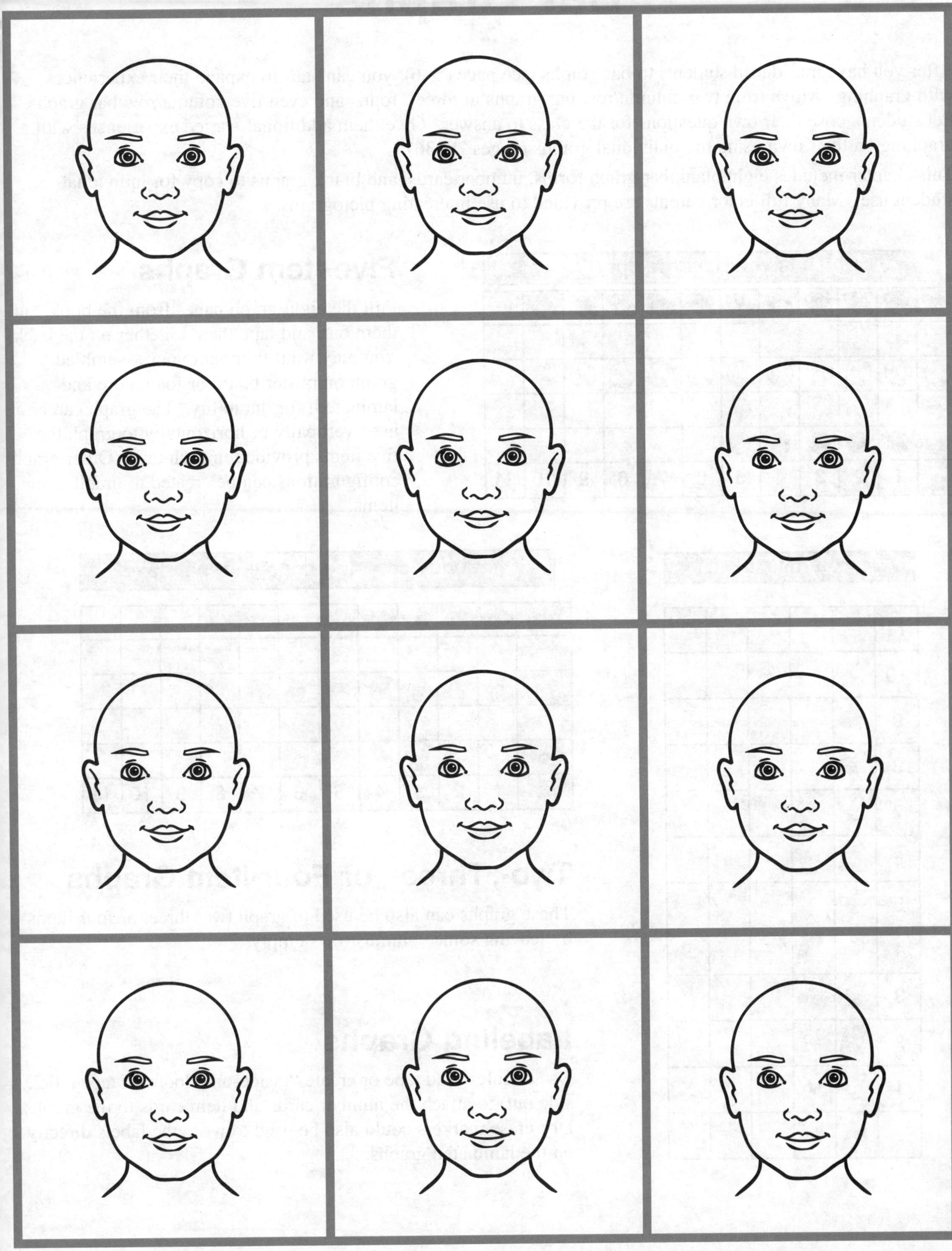

Bar Graphs

After you have introduced students to bar graphs (see pages 5–6), you can start to expand their experiences with graphing. Move from two-column/row bar graphs to three-, four-, and even five-column/row bar graphs. Let students pose their own questions for the class to answer. Give them additional, varied experiences with graphing on their own using the individual graphs (pages 29–36).

This chapter includes eight blank bar graph forms, number cards, and blank graphs to copy for individual student use. Many full-color cutouts are provided to use in creating pictograms.

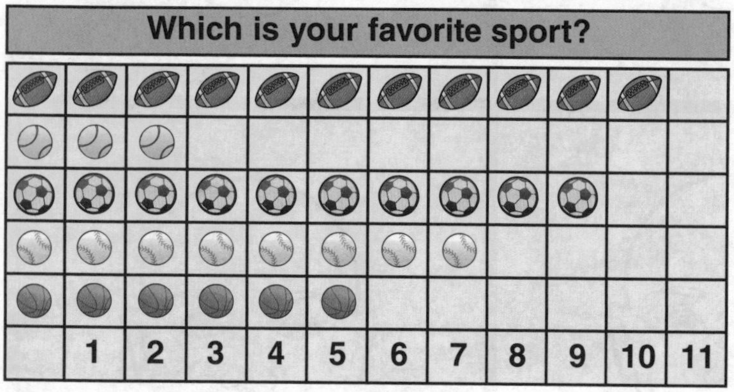

Five-Item Graphs

Pull the eight graph pages from the book, cut them out, and tape them together on the back. You may want to mount your assembled graph on poster board or foam core and laminate it for durability. The graph can be used vertically or horizontally to graph the five items provided in each unit. Other graph configurations can be created to graph more items.

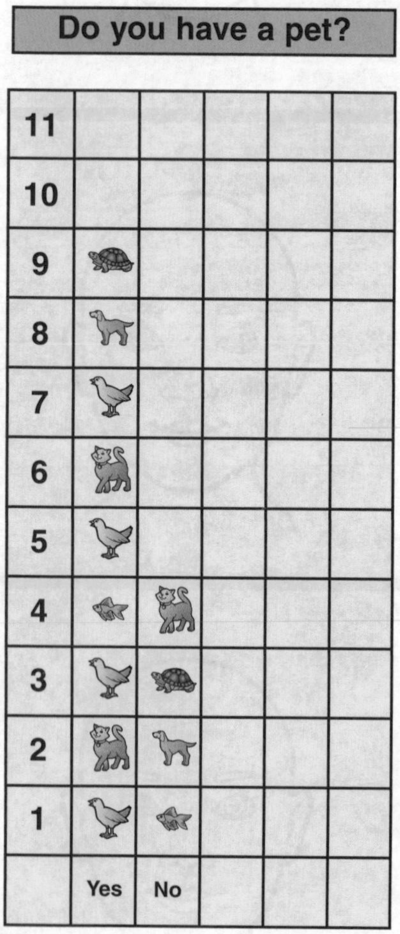

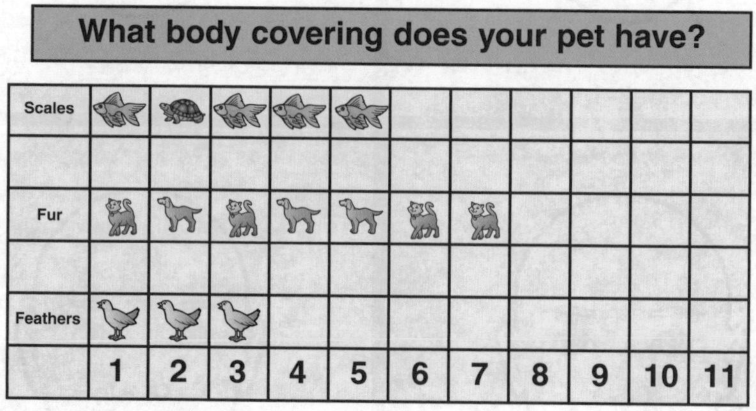

Two-, Three-, or Four-Item Graphs

These graphs can also be used to graph two, three, or four items by leaving some columns/rows empty.

Labeling Graphs

Use double-sided tape or create "inside-out" loops of tape (sticky side out) to attach the number cards and item cards to the graphs. Dry-erase markers could also be used to write the labels directly on the laminated graphs.

1	2	3
4	5	6
7	8	9
10	11	12

13	14	15
16	17	18
19	20	21
22	23	24

Name: ______________________________

Title:

8		
7		
6		
5		
4		
3		
2		
1		

Name: ____________________

Title:

	1	2	3	4	5	6	7	8

Name: ______________________________

Title:

8			
7			
6			
5			
4			
3			
2			
1			

Name: ____________________

Title:

	1	2	3	4	5	6	7	8

Name: ______________________________

Title:

8				
7				
6				
5				
4				
3				
2				
1				

Name: ______________________

Title:

	1	2	3	4	5	6	7	8

Name: ______________________________

Title:

8					
7					
6					
5					
4					
3					
2					
1					

Name: ____________________

Title:

1 2 3 4 5 6 7 8

Venn Diagrams

Venn diagrams are a wonderful way to help your students learn about the attributes of objects and how to sort them. A *Venn diagram* consists of two overlapping circles. Items are sorted into the two circles by one attribute (i.e., red shapes in the left circle; triangles in the right circle) and items that have both attributes are placed in the overlapping section (i.e., red triangles). Keep in mind, a Venn diagram works best with simple objects having clearly definable attributes, and that some items must share two attributes. Objects that do not have either attribute can be placed outside the circles (i.e., the green square).

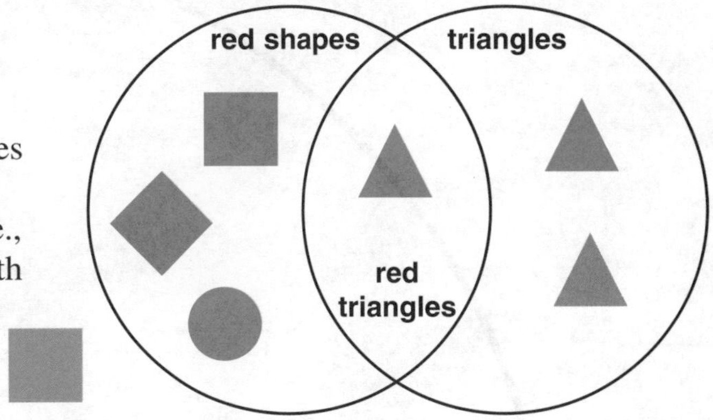

You can create a Venn diagram on the floor of your classroom using two hula hoops or loops of yarn. Start by laying out the two circles so that they are not touching or overlapping. Label one circle "lives in water" and the other "has four legs" using a sheet of paper, an index card, or a sentence strip. Ask students to help you sort the pet cutouts (pages 141–152). Hold up the dog, the cat, and the fish and for each pet, ask students, "Does it have four legs?" and "Does it live in the water?" Help students place each pet in the correct circle. When you show the bird, explain that it doesn't belong in either circle, so you will put it outside the circles.

Show the turtle last and ask the two questions. Allow some discussion, then show students how to overlap the circles and place the turtle in the overlapping section because it has four legs and it lives in the water. Ask students to think of other animals that have four legs and live in water. You could have them draw and cut out these animals and place them in the Venn diagram.

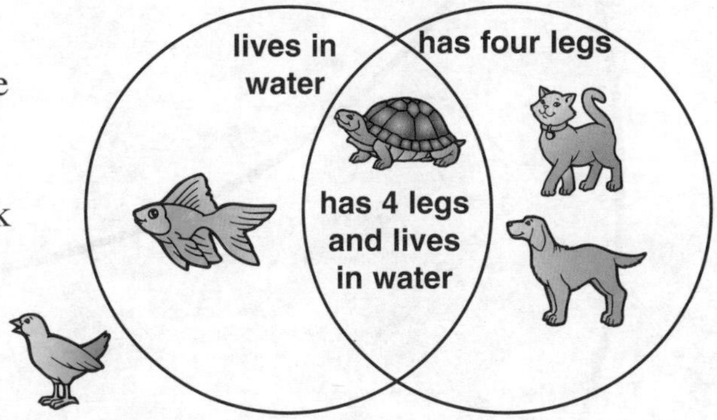

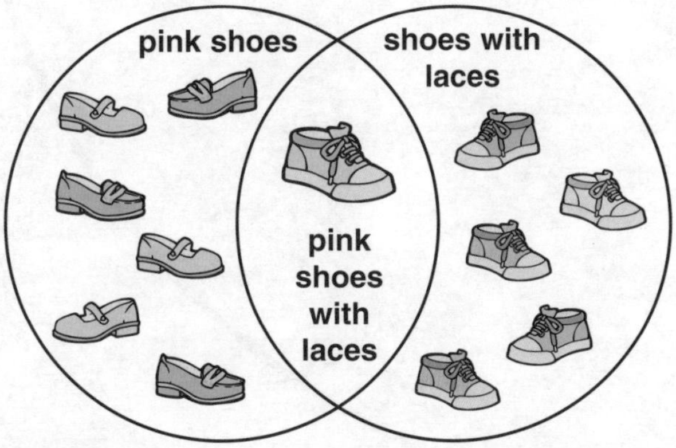

As a class or with a small group, continue to practice sorting using concrete objects (shoes, blocks, books, etc.), then transition to pictograms using the Venn diagram on pages 38–42. Students can cut out photos or illustrations from magazines or catalogs to sort, or use the full-color cutouts at the back of the book.

Provide individual practice by giving students copies of the individual Venn diagram (page 38) and letting them sort small items or math manipulatives. You can label the diagrams ahead of time or let more advanced students create their own labels.

Venn Diagram

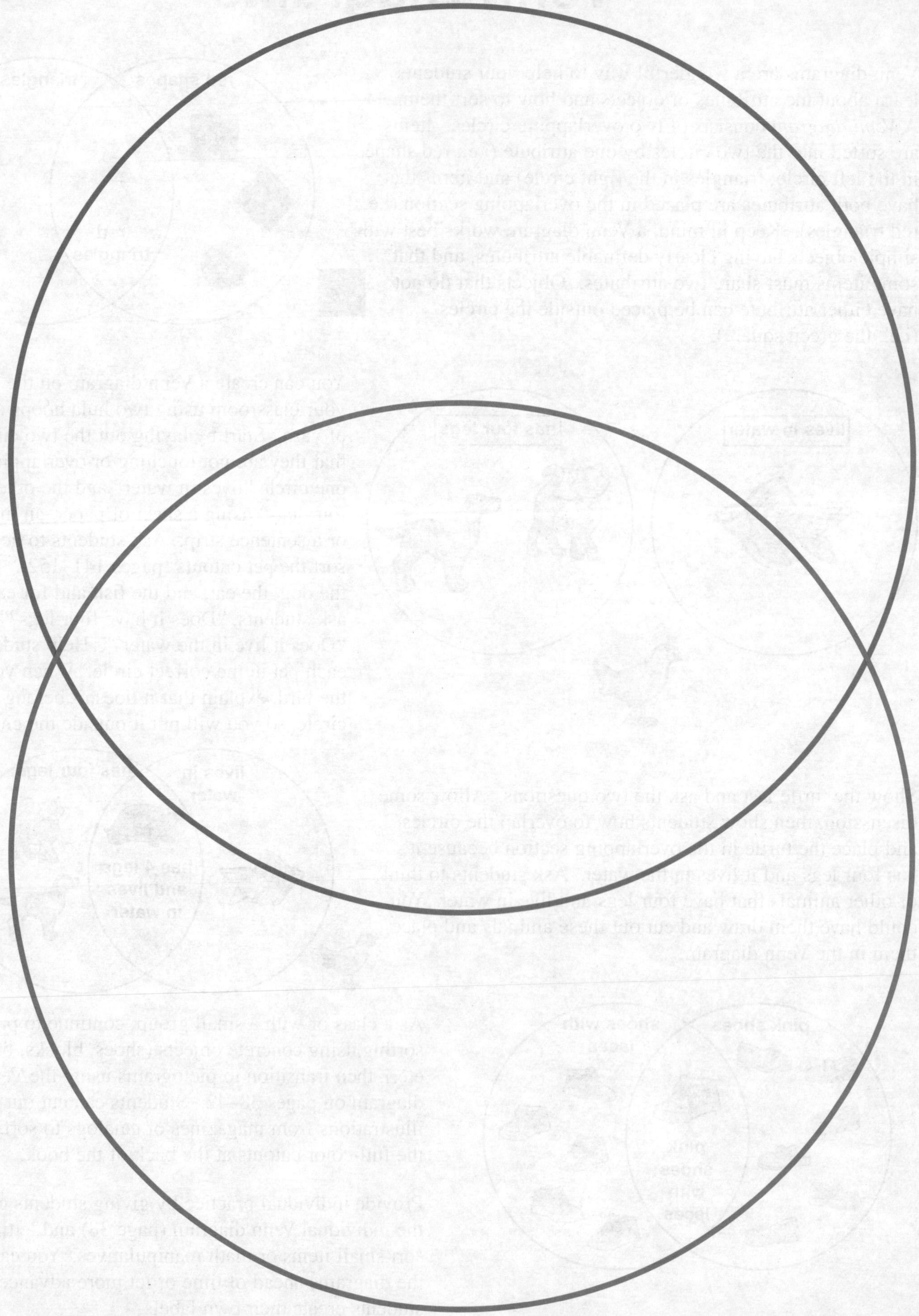

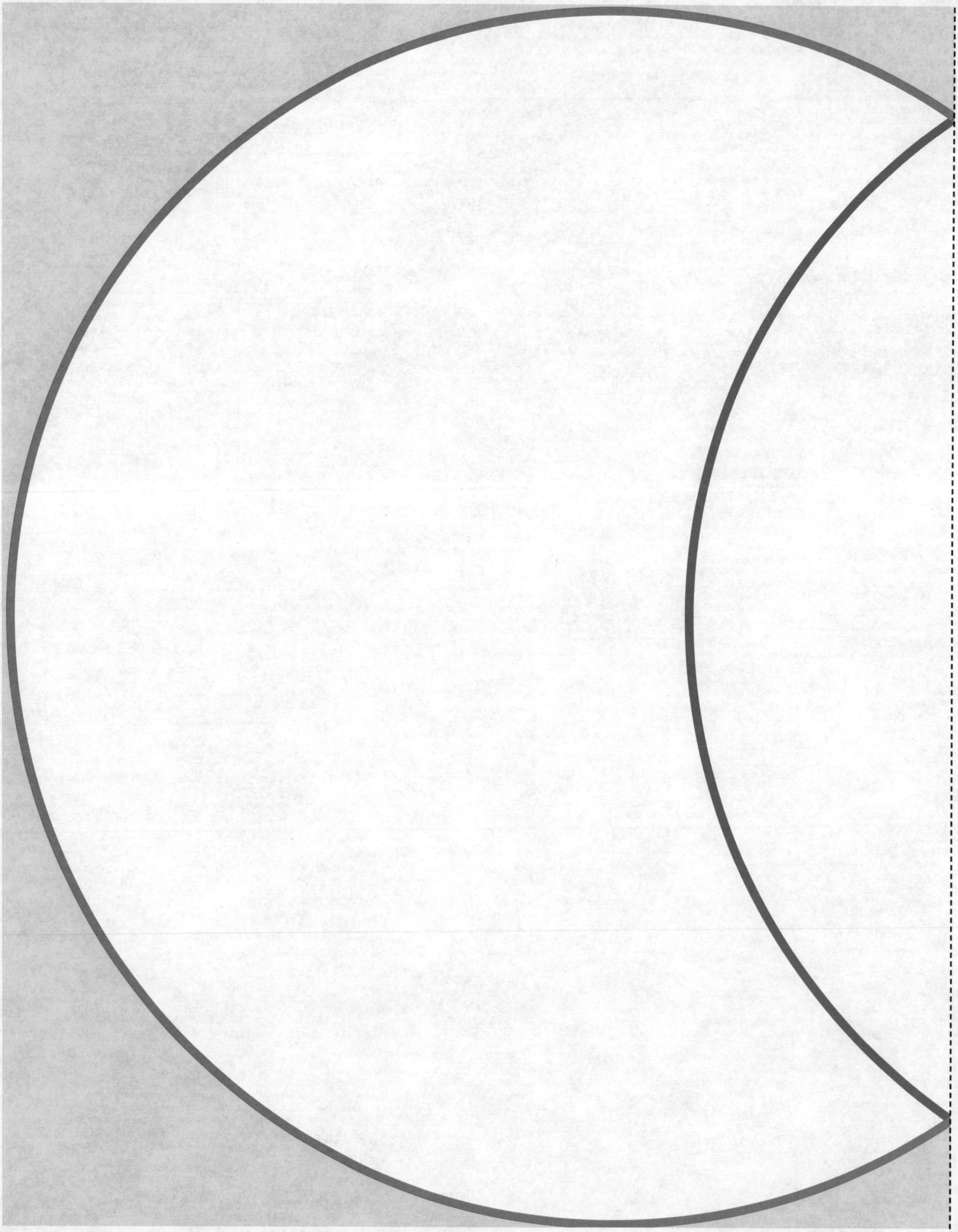

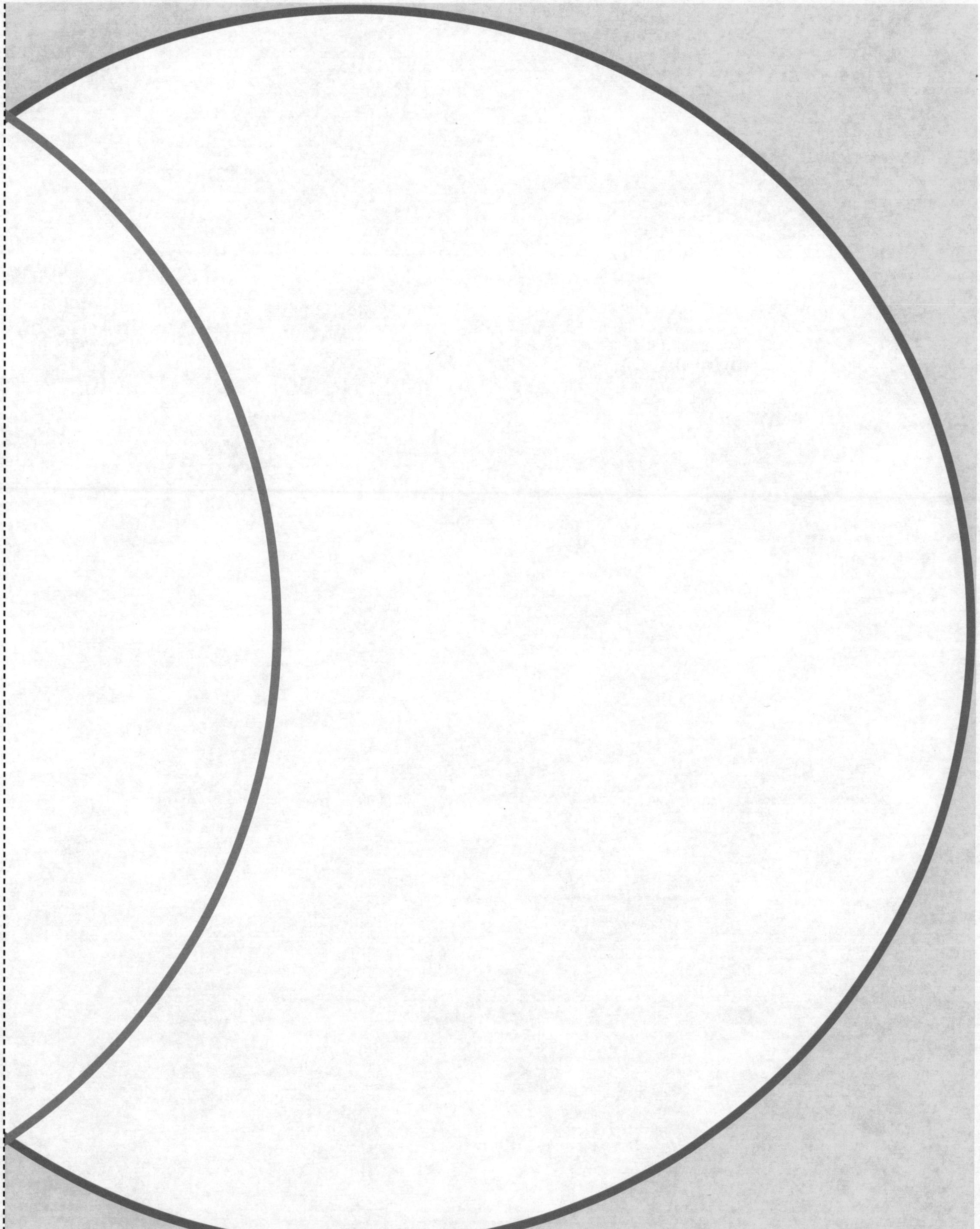

Pie Charts

Pie charts represent data as parts of a whole circle. The best way to introduce pie charts to young children is by using a circle that has already been divided into equal parts. Students can then graph the same number of items as there are sections on the chart. For example, the pull-out pie charts on pages 44–48 have 10 sections, so they should be used to graph 10 objects. Students often call these "pizza charts," as they are more familiar with pizza than pie.

The hardest thing for young students to understand about pie charts is that like items must be next to each other to form groups. To demonstrate, give each of 10 students an item to graph (in this case, pet cutouts from pages 141–152). Ask them to place their pets into the pie chart (pages 44–47), one pet in each section of the "pizza,". They will most likely place the cutouts randomly. Ask students to analyze the pie chart. Which pet is the most common? Is it easy to tell?

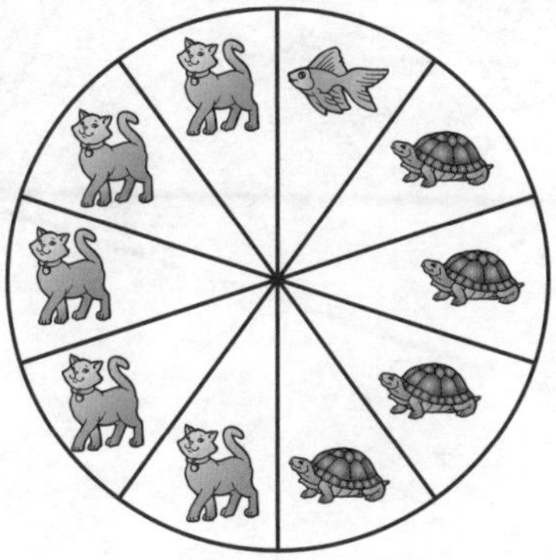

Then, show students how to arrange the items next to each other, so they form groups. Ask them to analyze the pie chart again. Is it easier to tell which pet is the most common? Then, on a separate pie chart, show them how to color in the sections, designating a color for each item (i.e., cat sections, red; fish sections, yellow; turtle sections, blue). Does this make the chart easier to read?

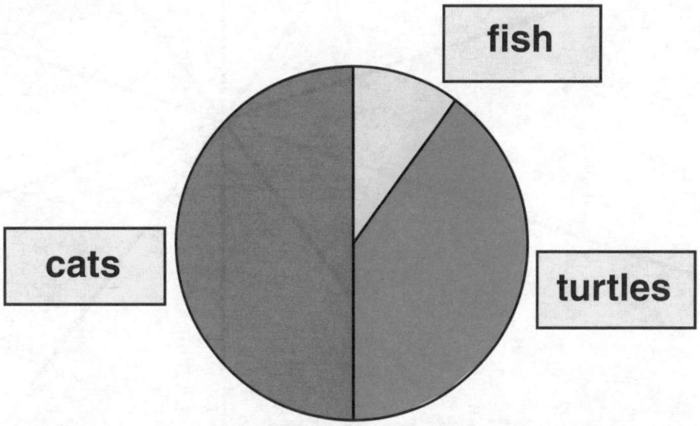

You can create a pie chart from data in a bar graph to show students that data can be organized and presented in multiple ways. You can also use data from a pie chart to create a bar graph. For example, have students use the pet cutouts in the pie chart above to create a bar graph, then compare the two graphs.

Individually, students can sort 10 items into a pie chart. In the example below, a student sorted 10 pattern blocks into the sections of the pie chart, then colored the sections to match the blocks.

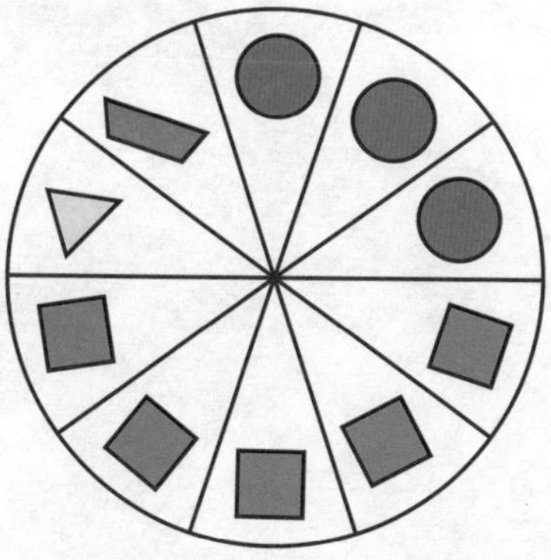

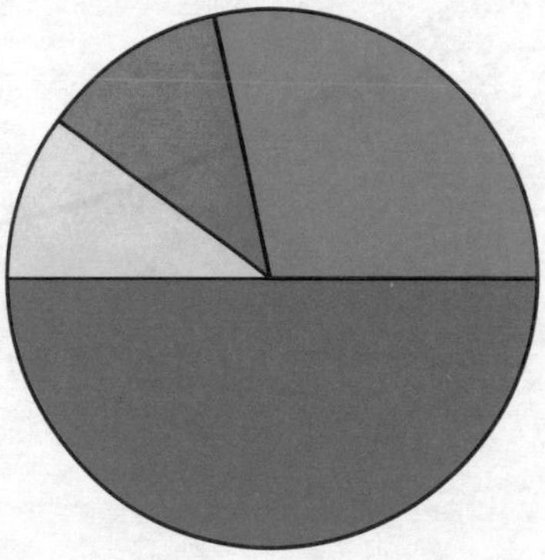

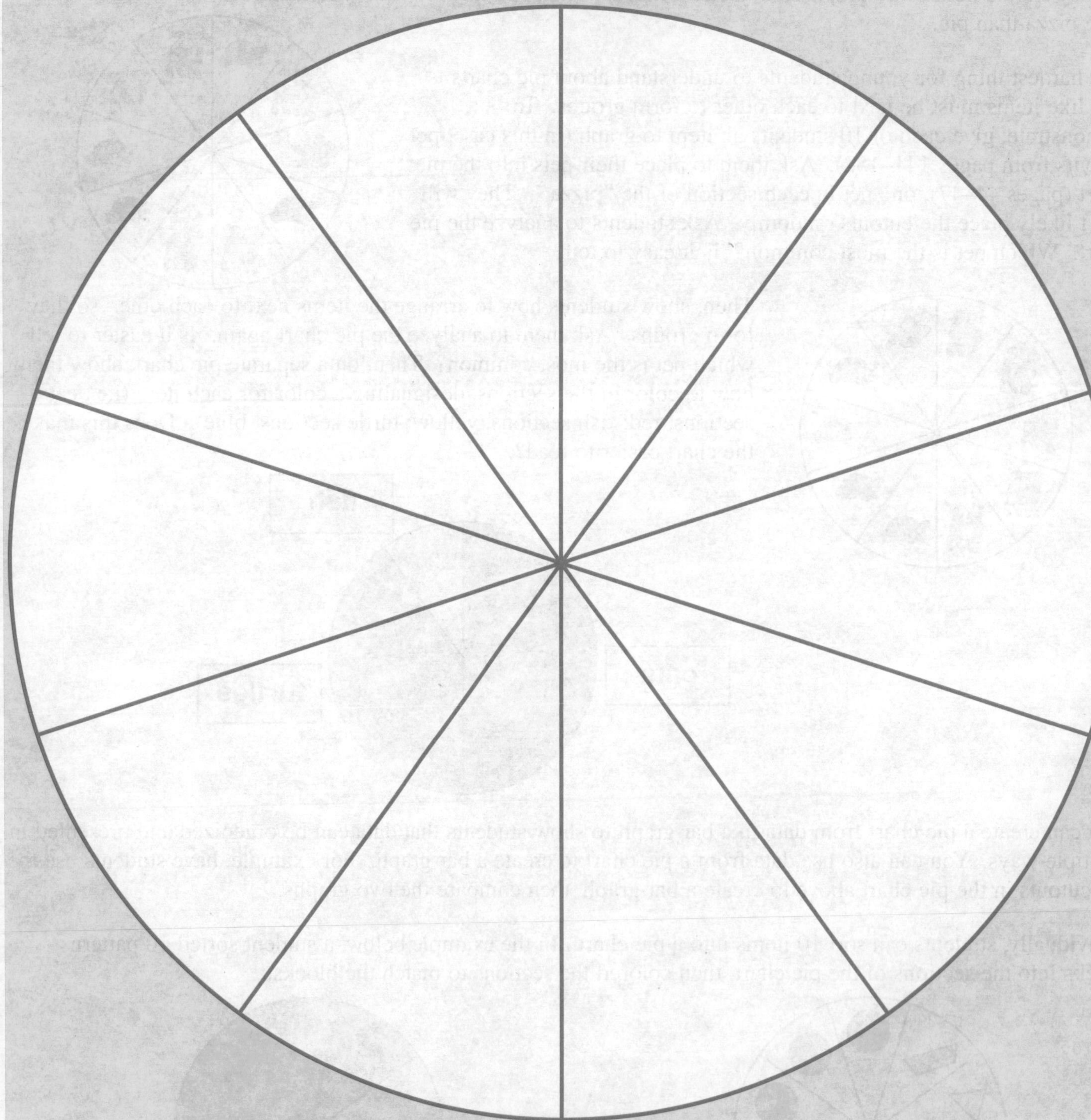

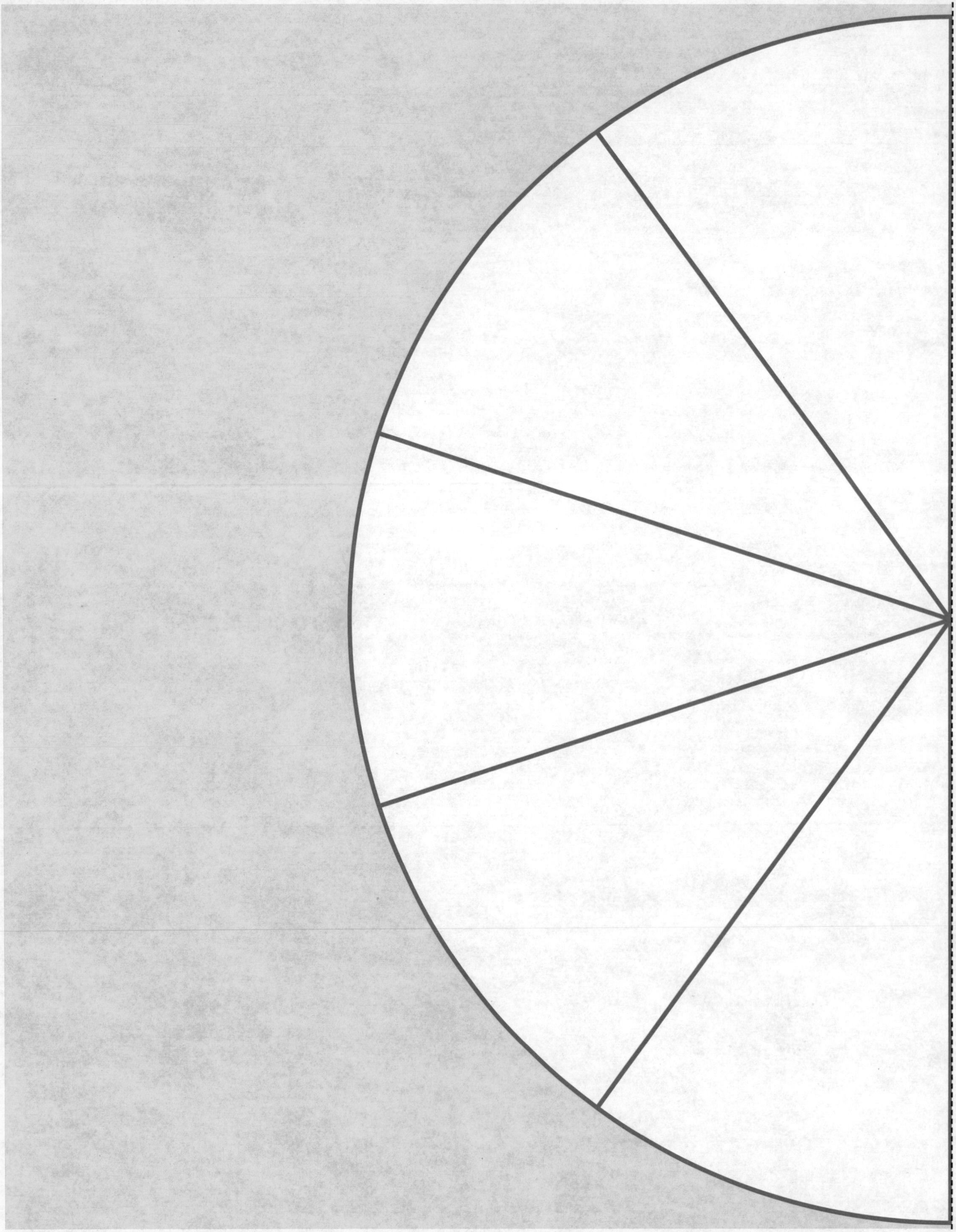

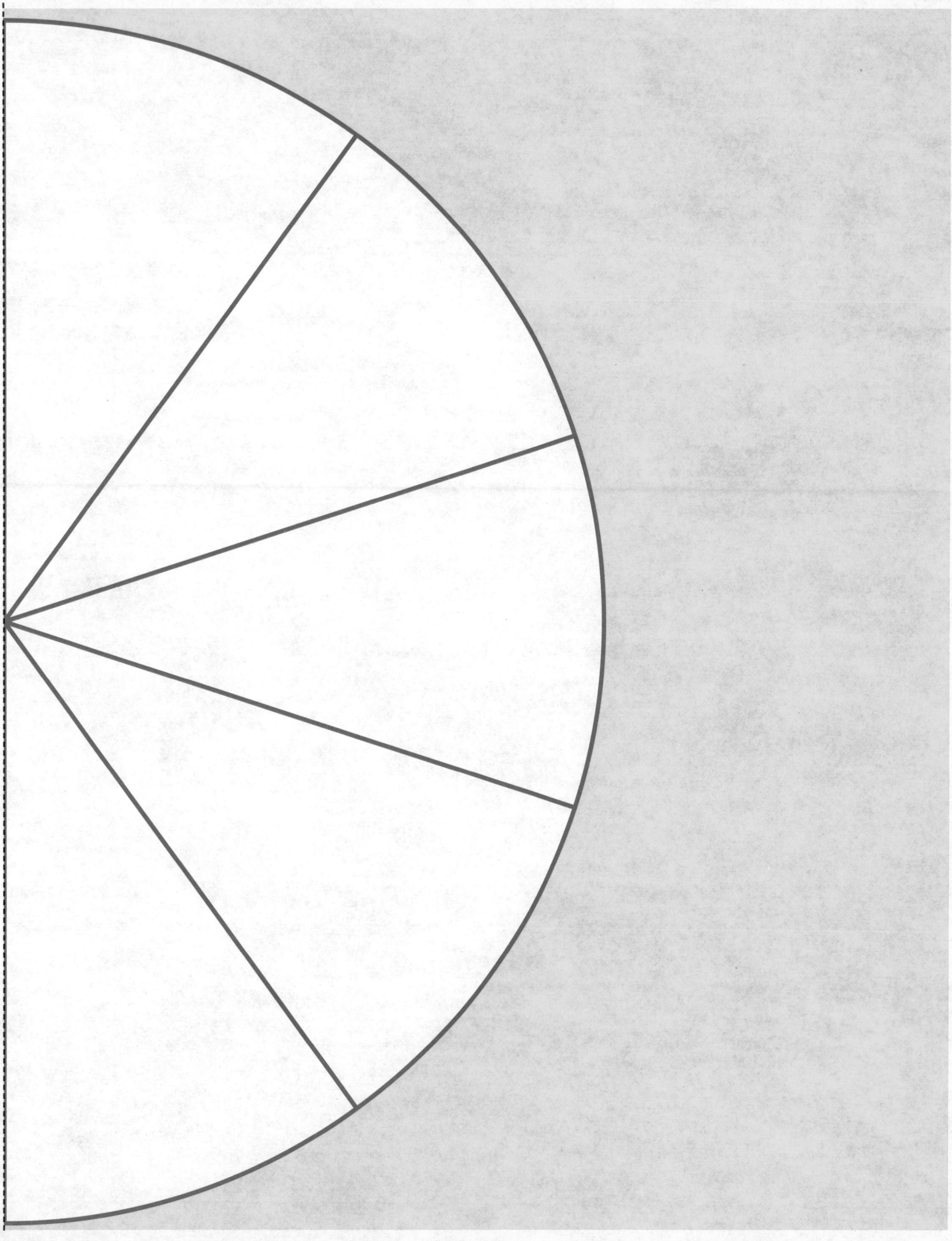

Line Graphs

Line graphs show change over time. This line graph shows the change in the daily temperature over one week. To create a weekly temperature graph, help students read and record the temperature each day. Show students how to locate the day at the bottom of the graph, then follow the line up with your finger to the correct temperature and make a dot. As you add a new dot each day, show students how to draw a line from yesterday's dot to today's. When analyzing a line graph, ask students to tell the "story" that the graph shows. For example, this graph shows that it got cooler on Wednesday and then grew warmer again through Friday.

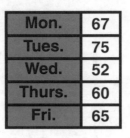

Mon.	67
Tues.	75
Wed.	52
Thurs.	60
Fri.	65

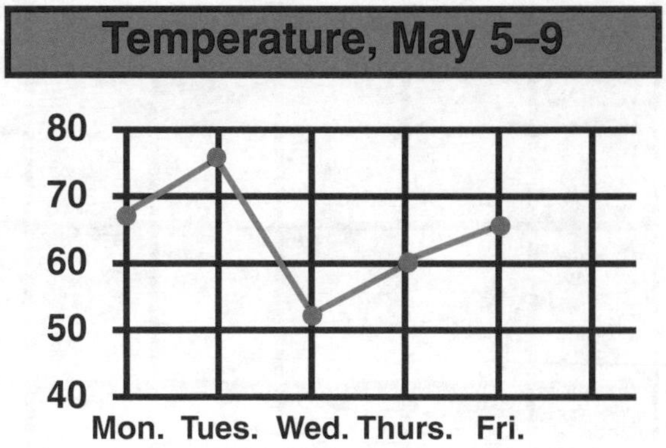

The line graph below shows the number of teeth lost in Mrs. Duncan's class during the school year. Each month, students who lost teeth wrote their names and the number of teeth they lost on a chart. At the end of each month, the class plotted the point on the graph with a tooth-shaped sticker and connected the line from the previous month's tooth. At the end of the year, the class told the story of the graph and the teacher posted it on the wall.

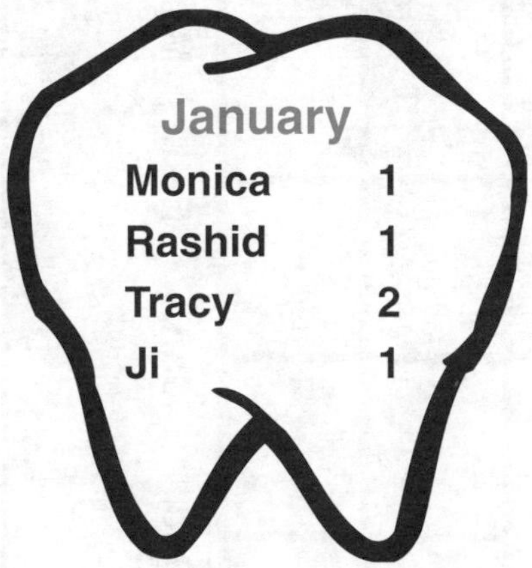

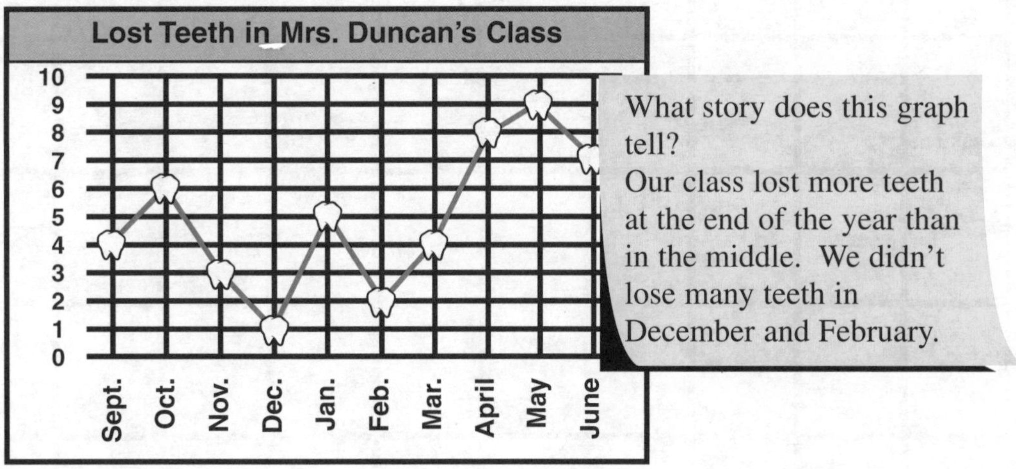

You can use line graphs to show anything that changes over time. As you evaluate students' knowledge of letter sounds, create individual line graphs showing the number of letters they recognize each month. They will enjoy seeing the line go up as the year progresses! You could also create individual line graphs (pages 50–53) to show the change in students' heights or shoe sizes by month. If you do a science experiment, such as growing plants, create a line graph to show the progress of your experiment.

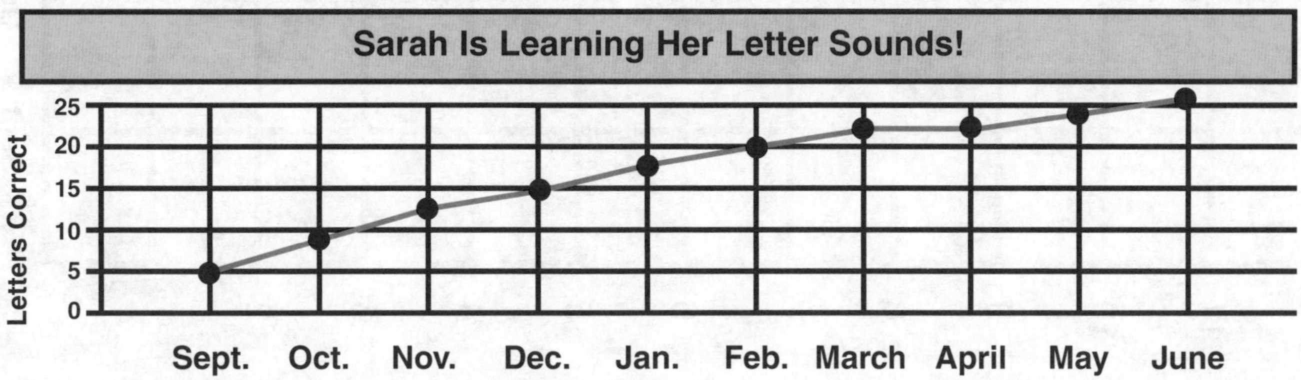

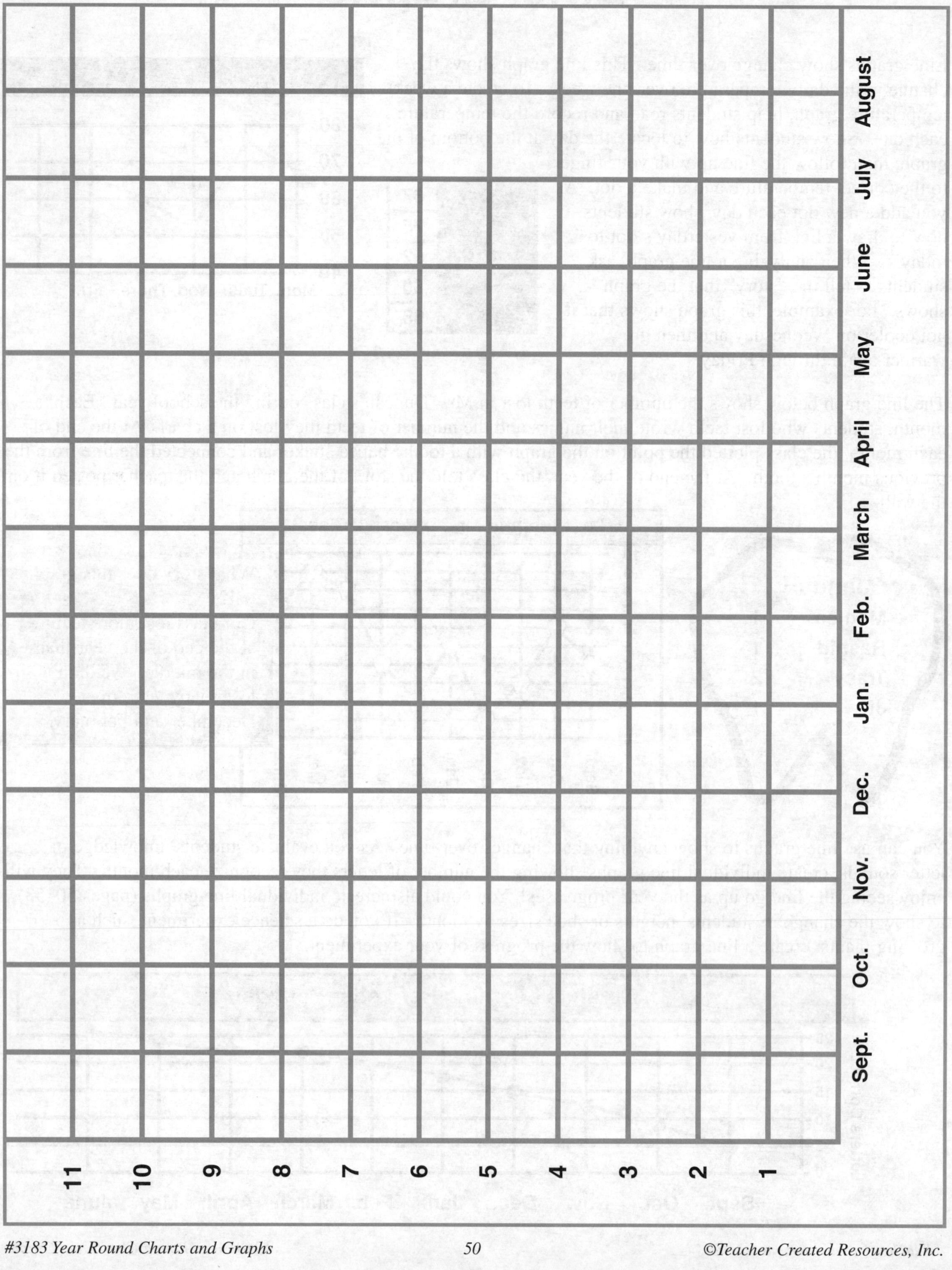
August
July
June
May
April
March
Feb.
Jan.
Dec.
Nov.
Oct.
Sept.
11
10
9
8
7
6
5
4
3
2
1

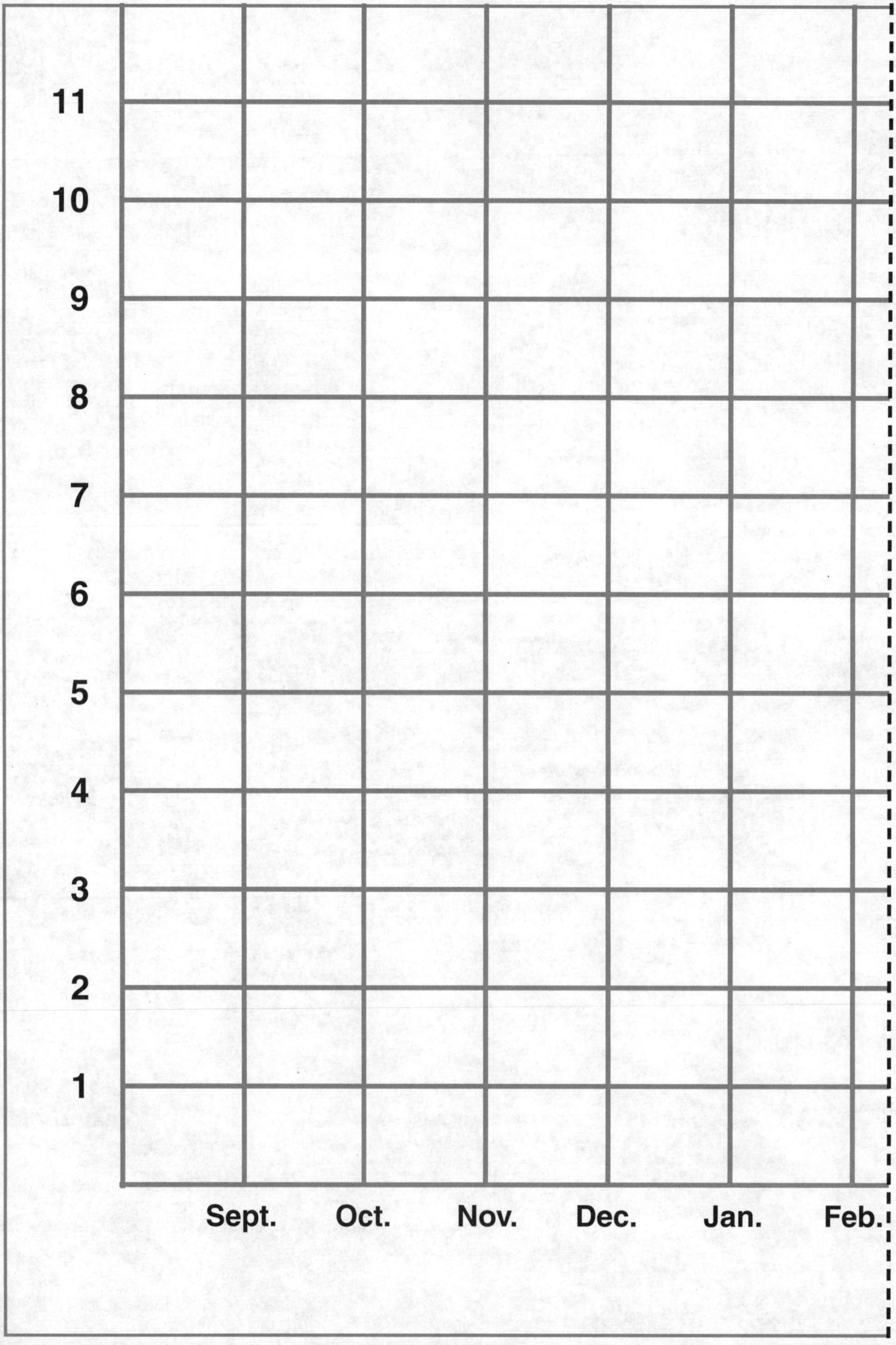
11
10
9
8
7
6
5
4
3
2
1
Sept.
Oct.
Nov.
Dec.
Jan.
Feb.

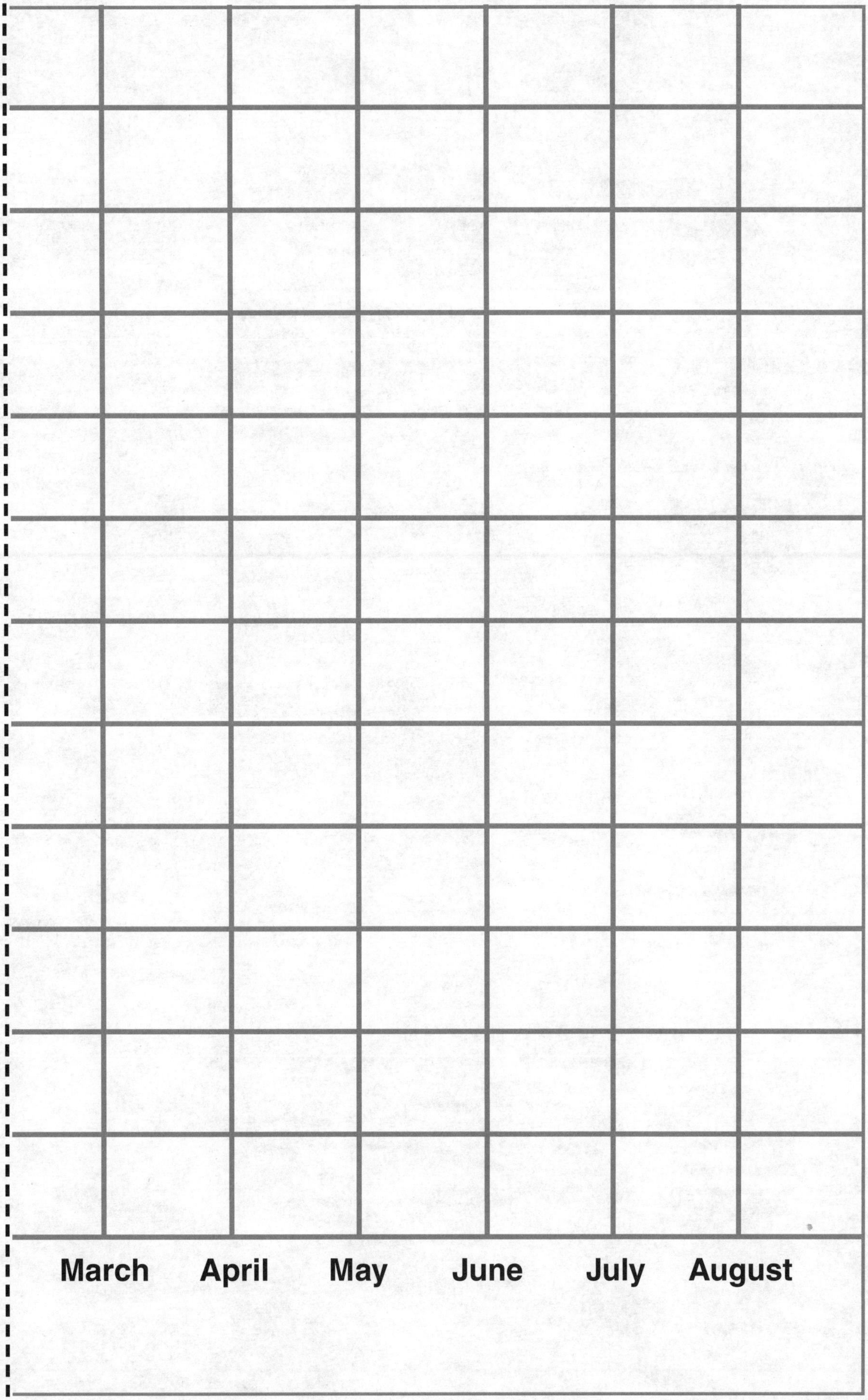
March
April
May
June
July
August

Graph and Chart Analysis Questions

After you create a graph or chart with your students, use these questions to help them analyze their data. Many of the questions can be adjusted or extended to fit the specific graph you are analyzing.

Analyzing Any Graph or Chart

What can you tell by looking at this graph?

What information does this graph show?

What story does this graph tell?

Analyzing Bar Graphs

Which column/row has the most?

Which was second? How many are in that one?

Is that more than the number in the______ column/row? How many more?

How many students chose______?

How many more students chose______than______?

Which column/row had the least?

How many fewer in the_____ column/row than in the______column/row?

Suppose two more students had chosen______. How would the graph have been different? Why do you think that is so?

Analyzing Venn Diagrams

Describe the objects that go in this circle.

What would an object be like that would go in this section?

Why did you put that object in that section?

Why doesn't this object go in that area?

Can you name an object that goes outside both circles?

Analyzing Pie Charts

Can you tell which section is the largest? Which section is the smallest? What does that tell us?

Were there more_____than_____? How can you tell?

Analyzing Line Graphs

What story does this line graph tell?

Do you notice any places where the line went way up or way down? Why do you think that is?

Did the line go up or down over the whole time? What does that tell you?

Sticky Note Labels

You can add labels to your charts and graphs using sticky notes. At first, you can record students' responses and stick them to the graph or chart. Later, you may want to let students add their own labels.

Which is your favorite sport?

More kids liked football than tennis.
Our class liked soccer the most.
Four kids voted for basketball.
1
2
3
4
7
8
9
10
11

Graphing Topics

Need some ideas for graphs? Here are a few—you will probably think of many more! There are also graphing topics on the first page of each unit in the Cutouts section beginning on page 57.

General Questions

- Do you like to _______?
- Do you have ________?
- Have you been to ________?

"Favorite" Suggestions—What is Your Favorite ___________?

- after school activity
- color
- flower
- ice cream
- lunch or snack
- pet
- season
- song
- sport
- story character
- TV show
- type of weather

Personal Questions

How many boys are in our class?
How many girls are in our class?
What season is your birthday in?
What time do you go to bed?
Did you bring your snack in a lunchbox or a bag?
What color are your eyes?
What color is your hair?
Are you right-handed or left-handed?
How many people are in your family?
How old are you?
How do you get home from school?
How do your shoes stay on?
(Velcro, laces, slip-on, buckle)
How many languages do you speak?
Are your sleeves long or short?
How many pockets are on your clothes?
How many letters (or vowels) are in your name?
What flavor birthday cake do you want this year?
Do you like to draw/write with a crayon, marker, or pencil?

Long-Term Line Graphs

- lost teeth
- weather
- temperature
- height
- shoe size
- plant growth

Seasonal Graphs

Fall: What did you do this summer?
Types of fallen leaves gathered outside
Candy wrappers from Halloween

Winter: Do you like to build snowmen or have snowball fights?
What holidays do you celebrate?
What part of a gingerbread man do you bite first?

Spring: Choose your favorite color egg.
What is your favorite spring animal (bunny, chick, lamb)?
Which seed do you think will sprout first?

Summer: Do you like to swim at the beach or in a pool?
Do you wear sunscreen?
Are you going on vacation?

Items to Sort and Graph

beads or sequins
blocks
bottle caps
candies
cereals
crackers

leaves
letter or number cards
math manipulatives
paper die-cuts
rocks or pebbles
seeds

shells
small toys (cars, dolls)
stamps
stickers
writing instruments

Farm Animals

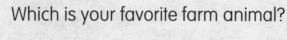

Graph Questions

Which is your favorite farm animal?

Which farm animal would you like to have for a pet?

Can you ride your favorite farm animal? (Yes/No)

Do you eat eggs? (Yes/No)

Do you like regular milk or chocolate milk?

Does it have fur, feathers, or hair?

What kind of eggs do you like to eat?

Have you been to a farm? (Yes/No)

Cow

Horse

Pig

Chicken

Sheep

Yes

No

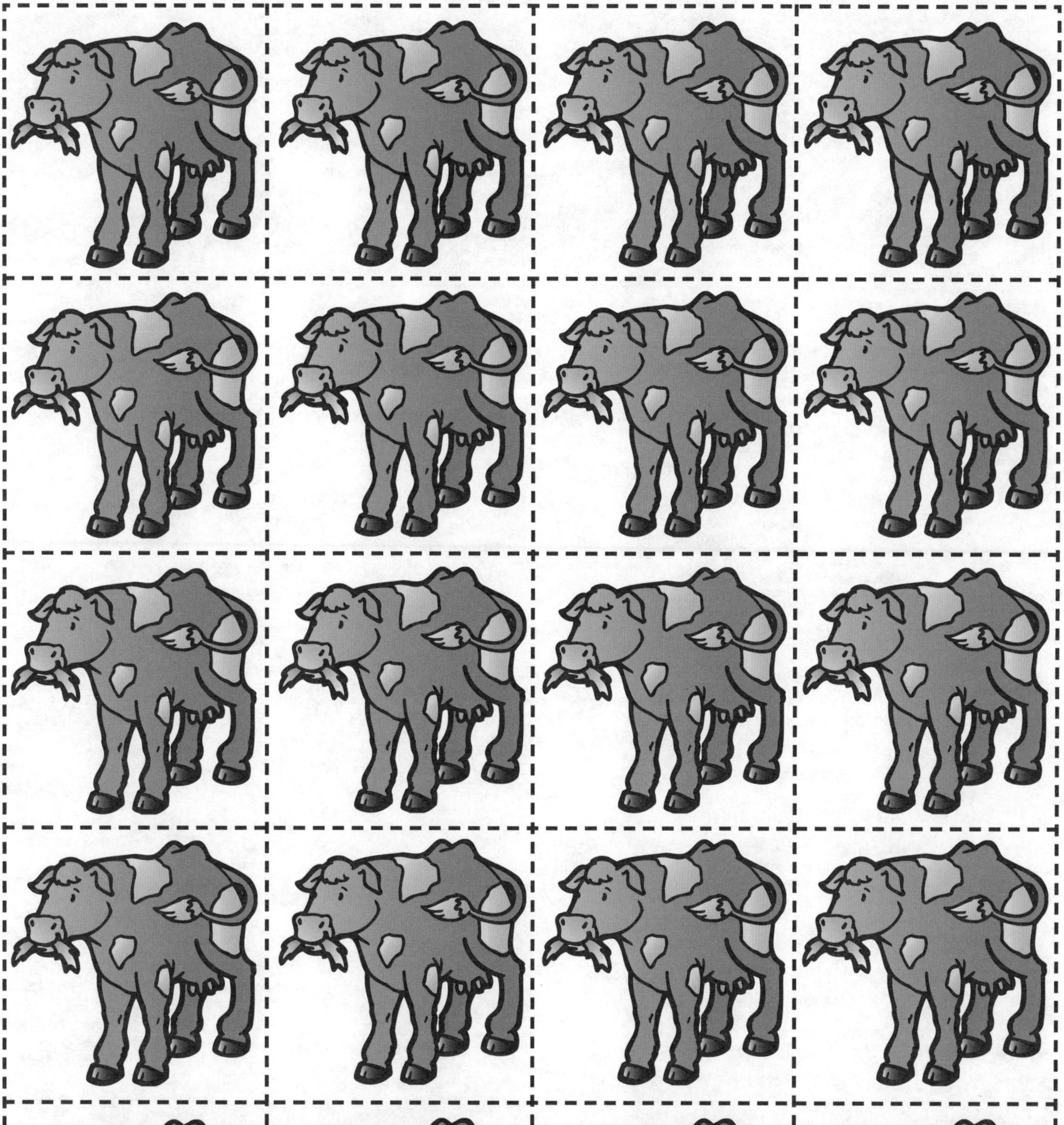

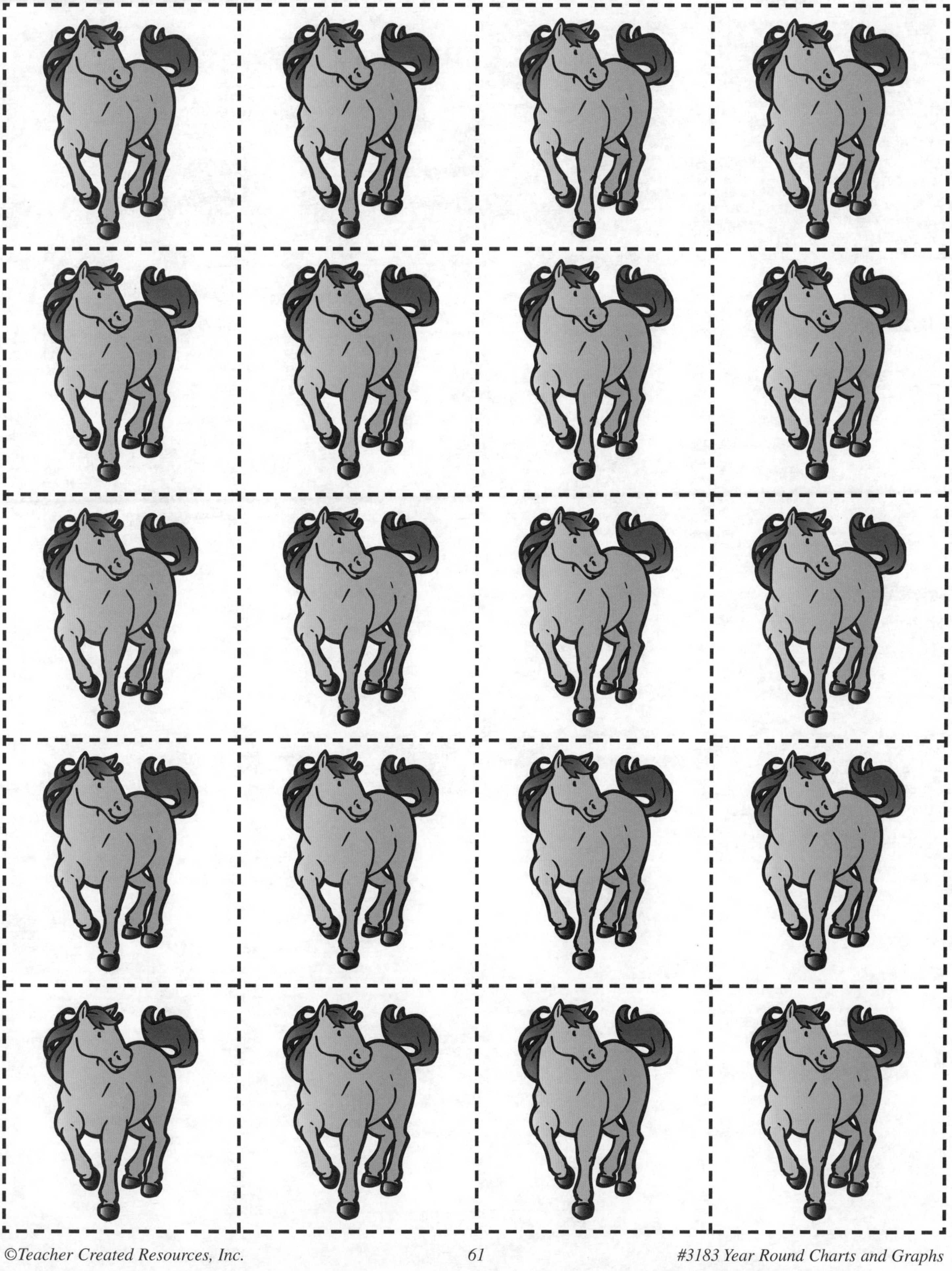

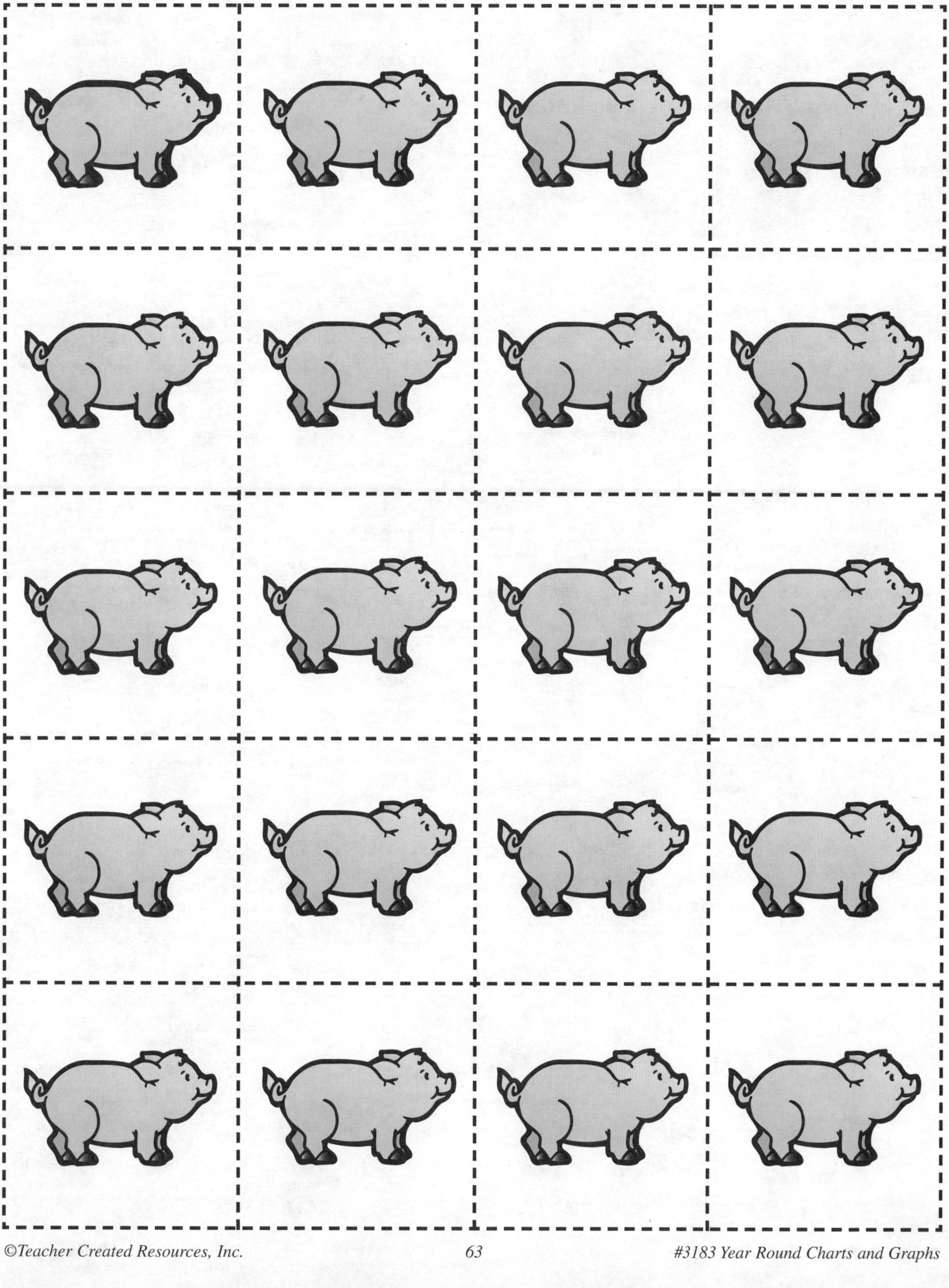

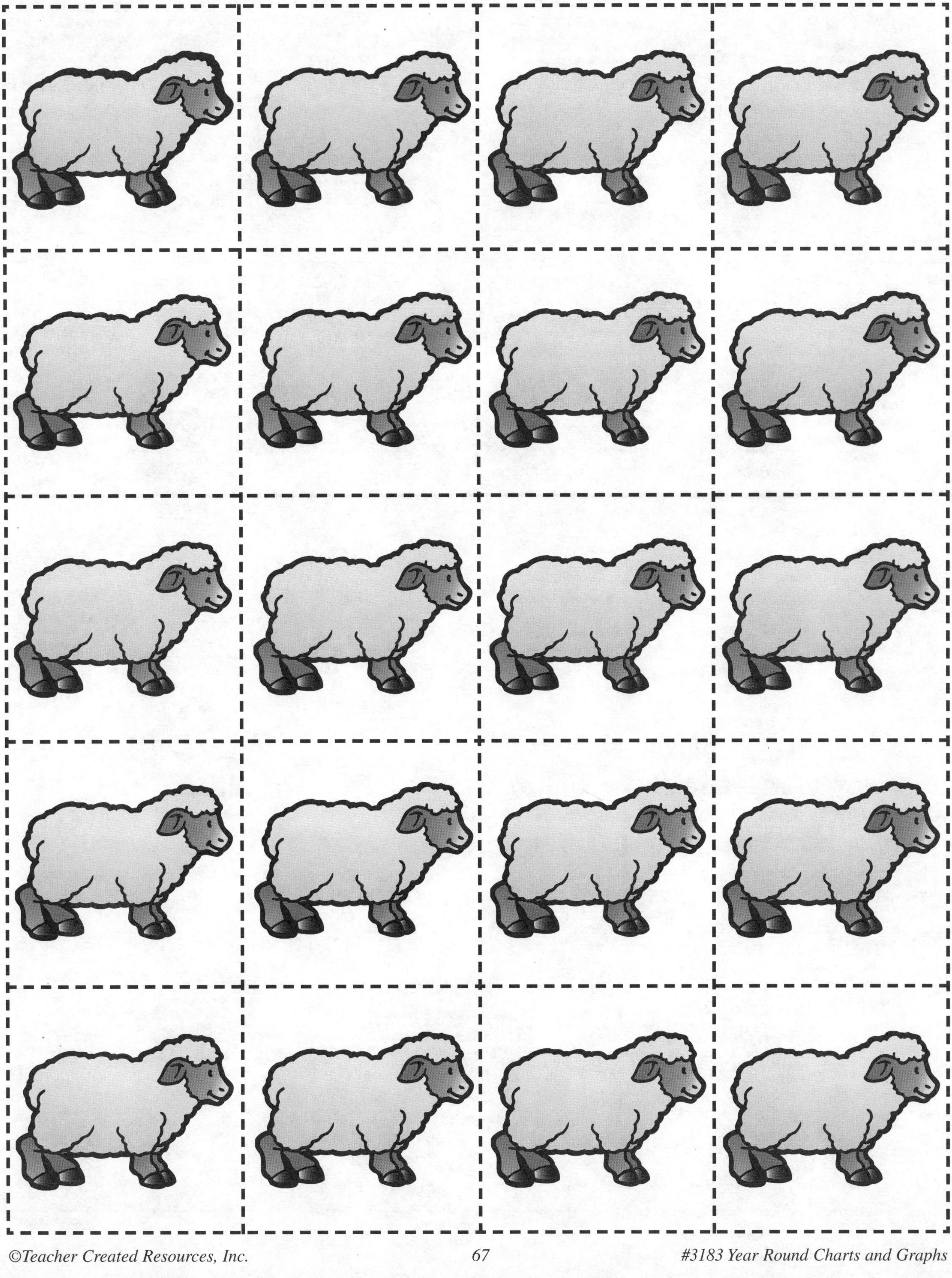

Sea Animals

Graph Questions

Which is your favorite sea animal?

Which sea animal would you like to have for a pet?

Does it swim? (Yes/No)

Does it have legs or fins?

Does it have lungs or gills?

Have you ever been to the beach/ocean? (Yes/No)

Fish

Shark

Octopus

Sea Star

Seal

Yes

No

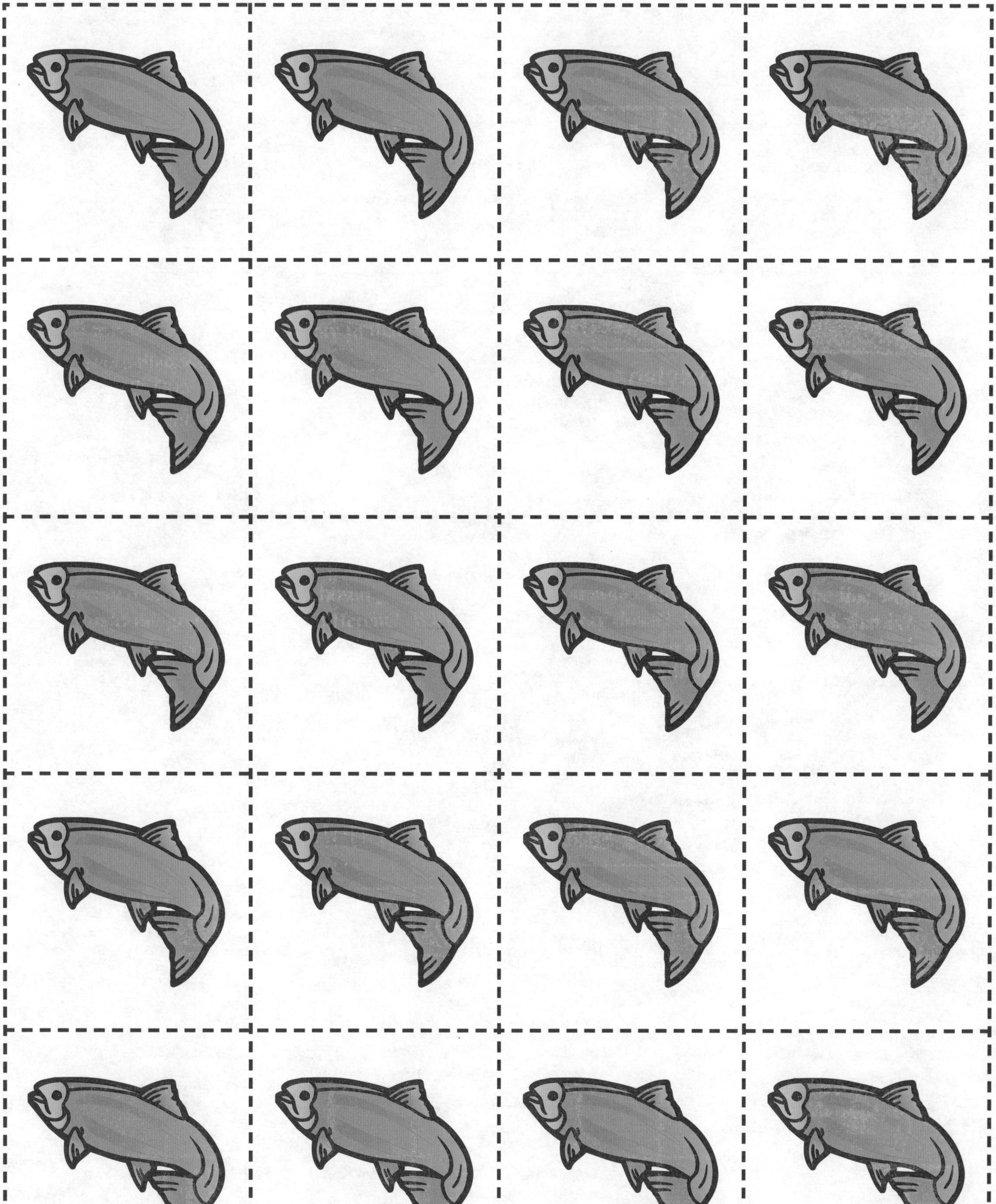

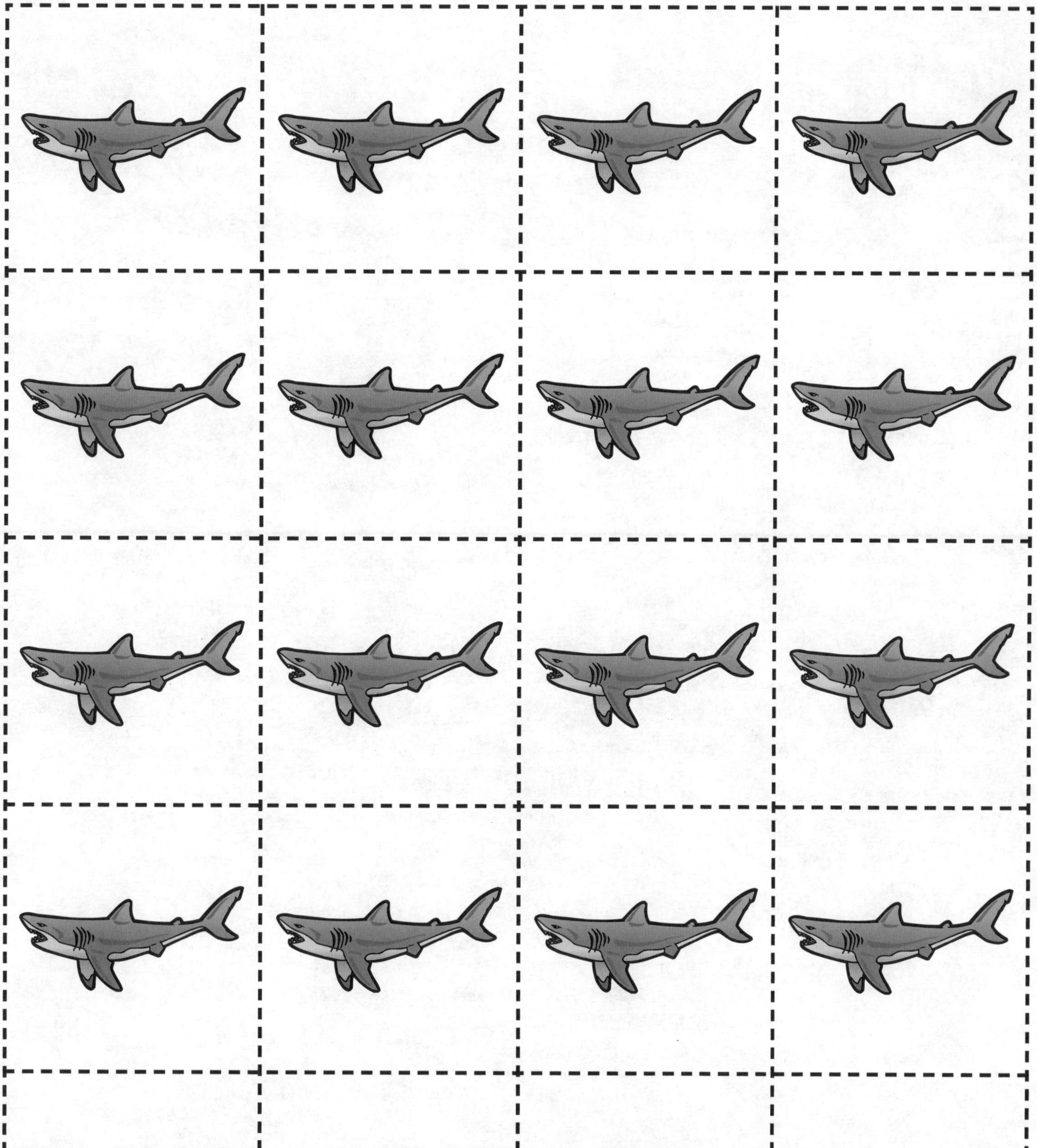

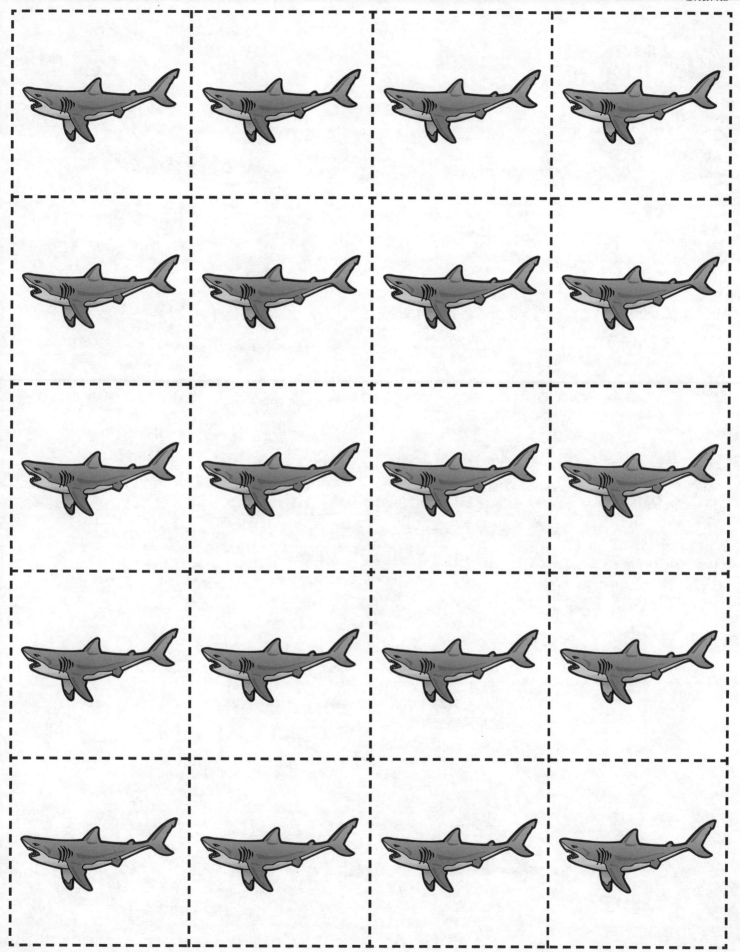

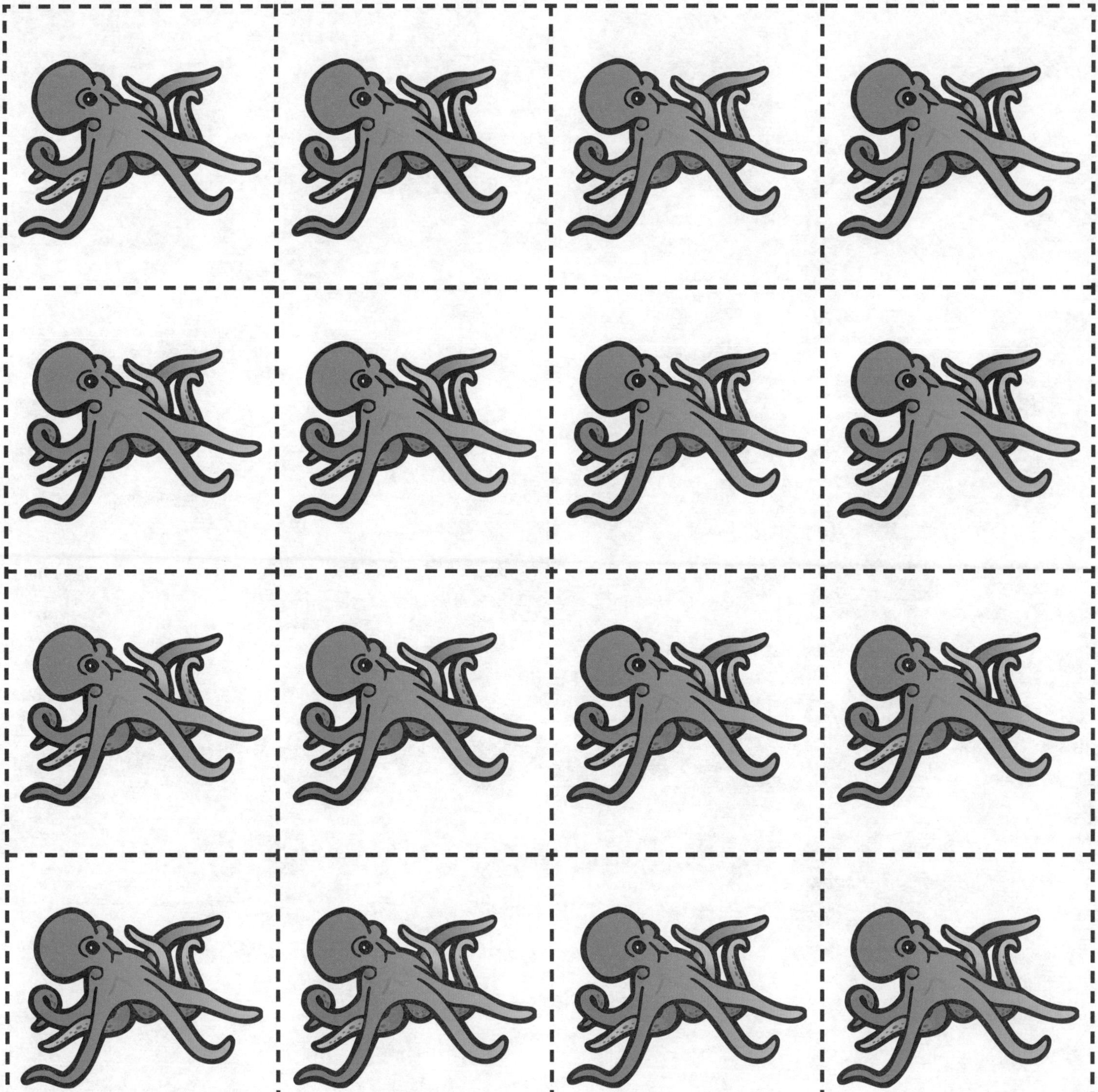

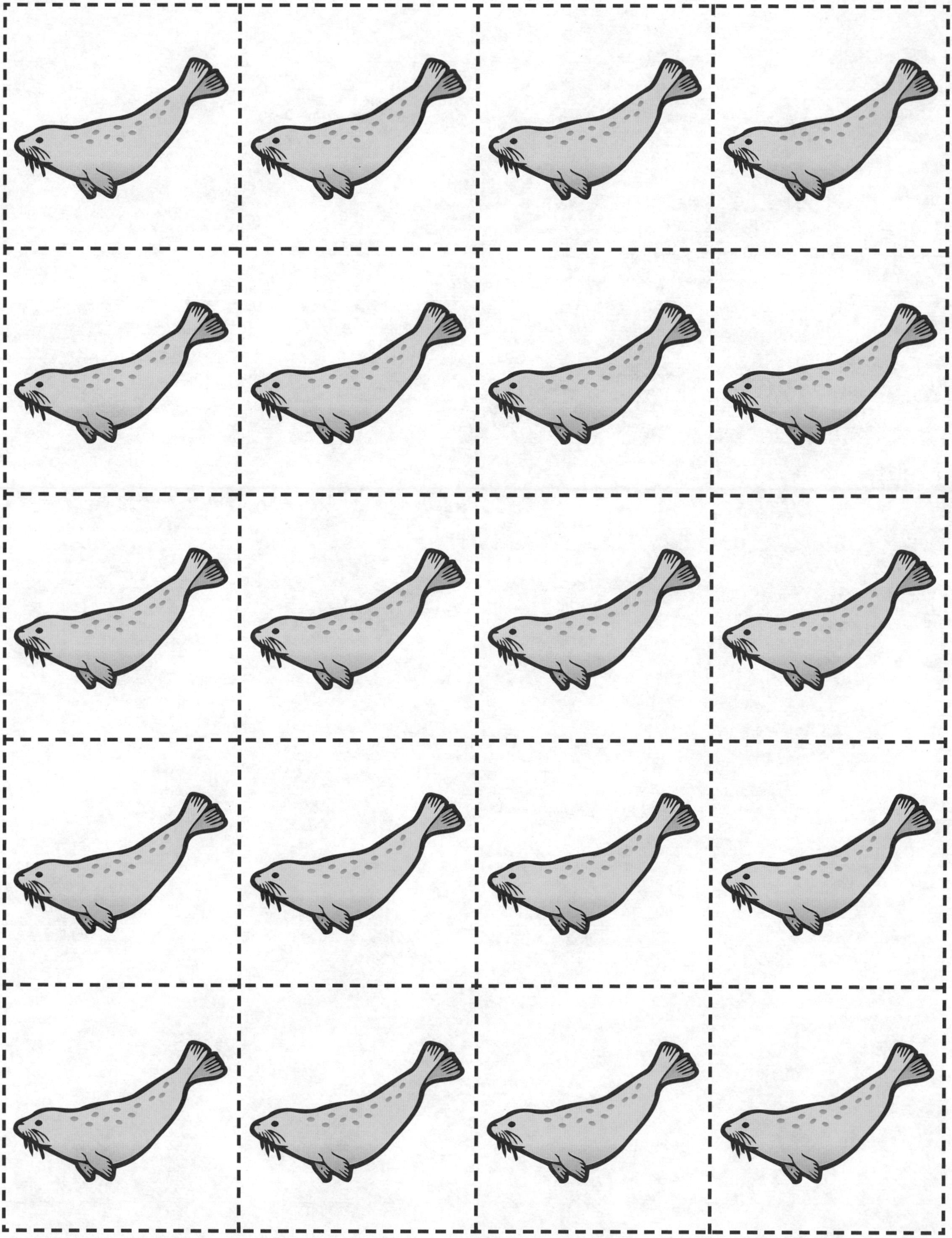

Creepy Crawlies

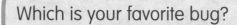

Graph Questions

Which is your favorite bug?

Do you like bugs? (Yes/No)

Which bug would you like to hold?

Does the bug fly? (Yes/No)

Does it have six, eight, or no legs?

Is it just one color or more than one color?

Ant

Butterfly

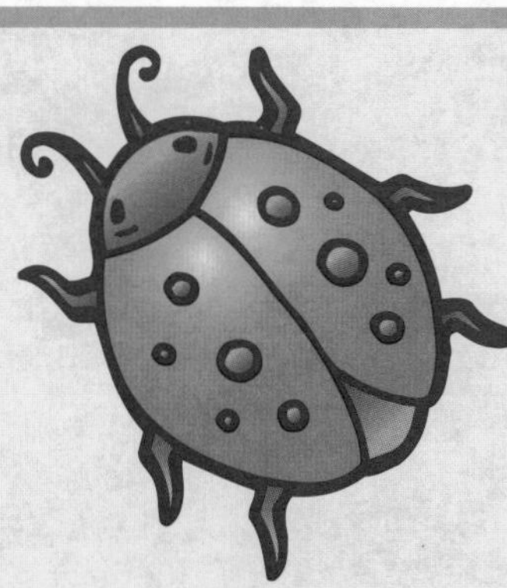

Ladybug

Spider

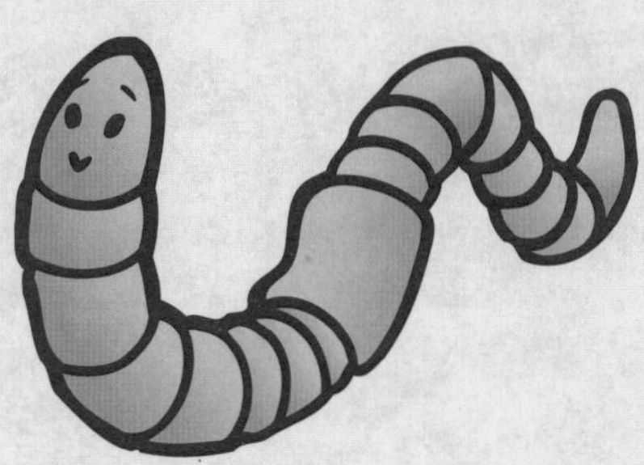

Earthworm

Yes

No

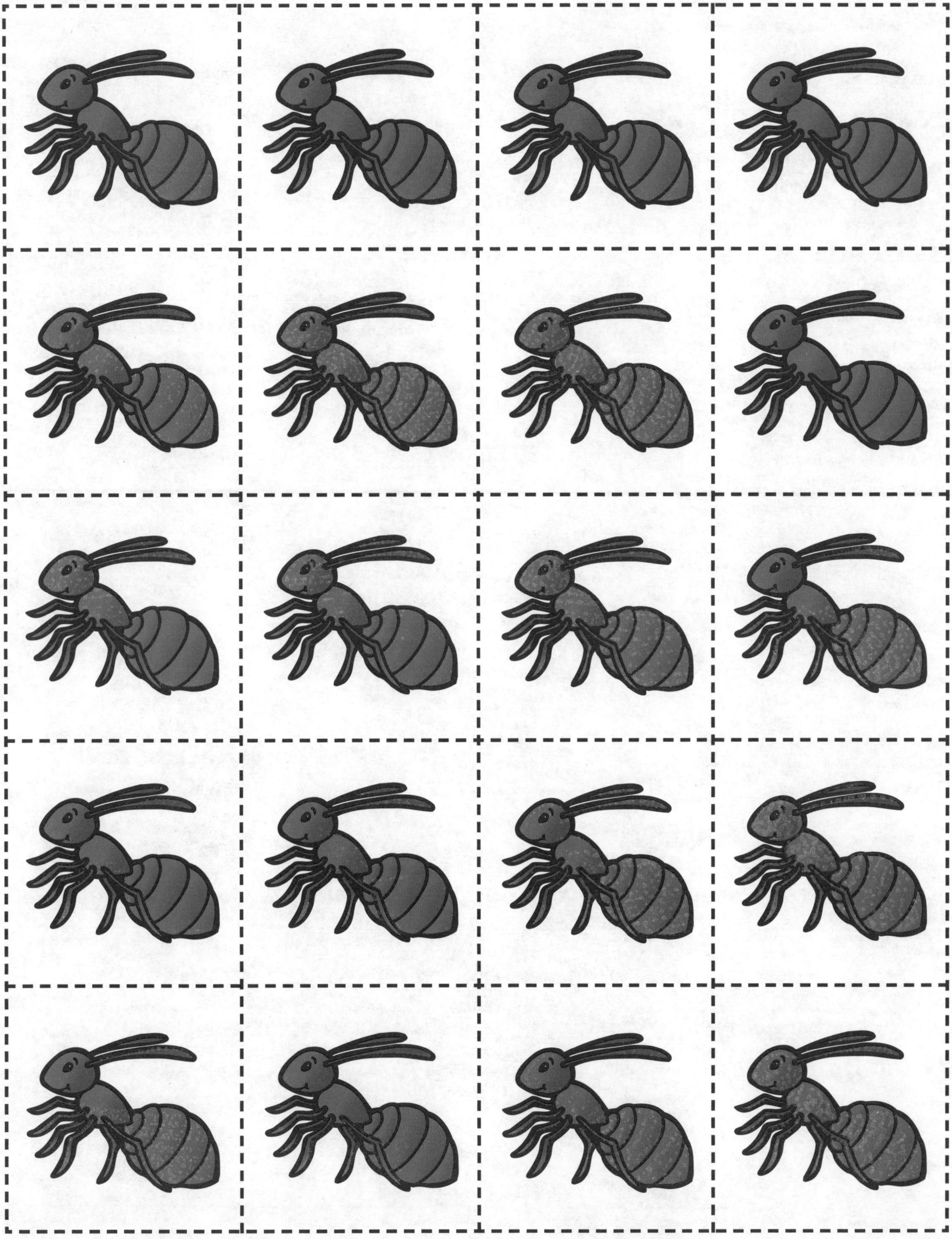

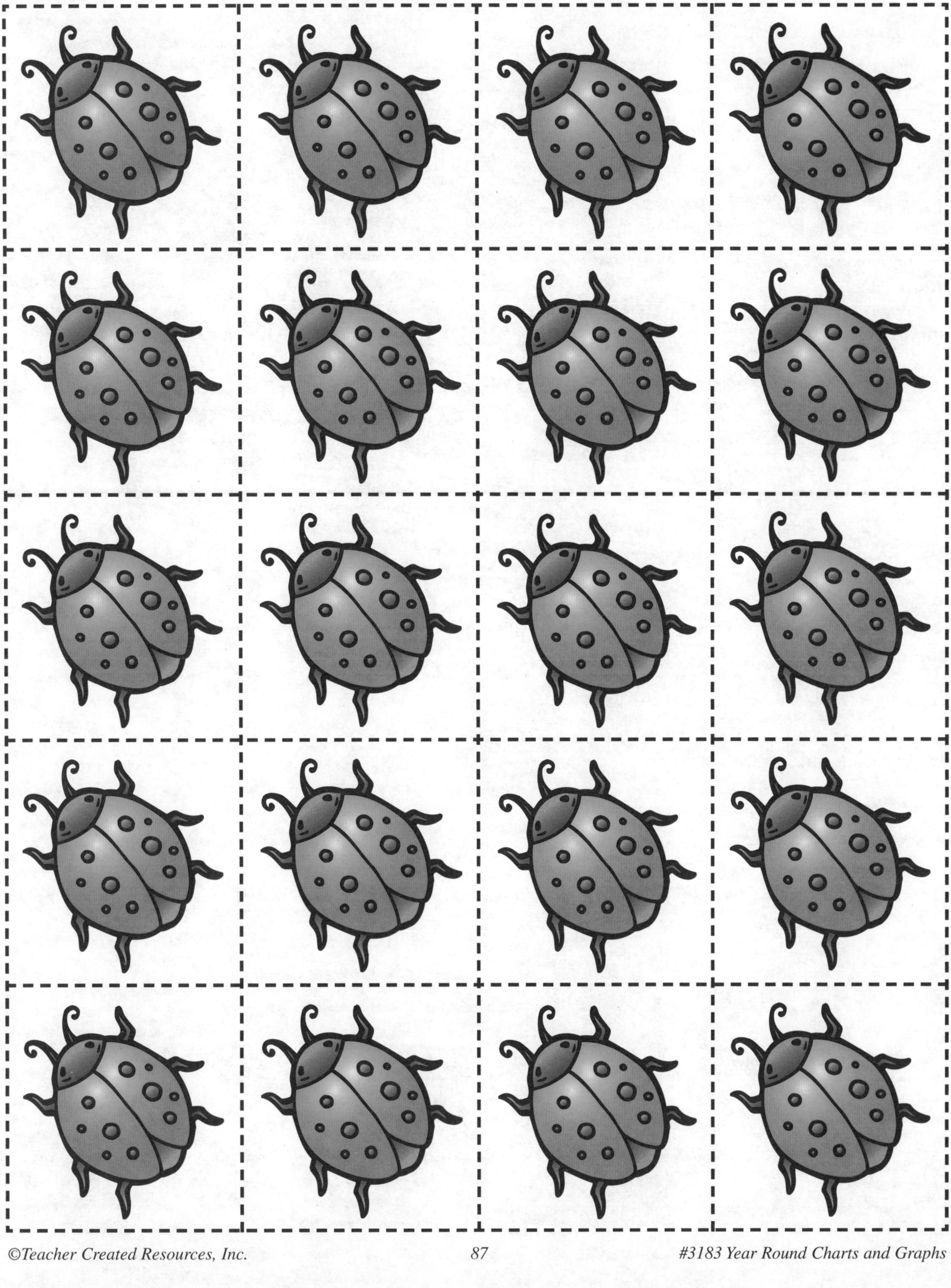

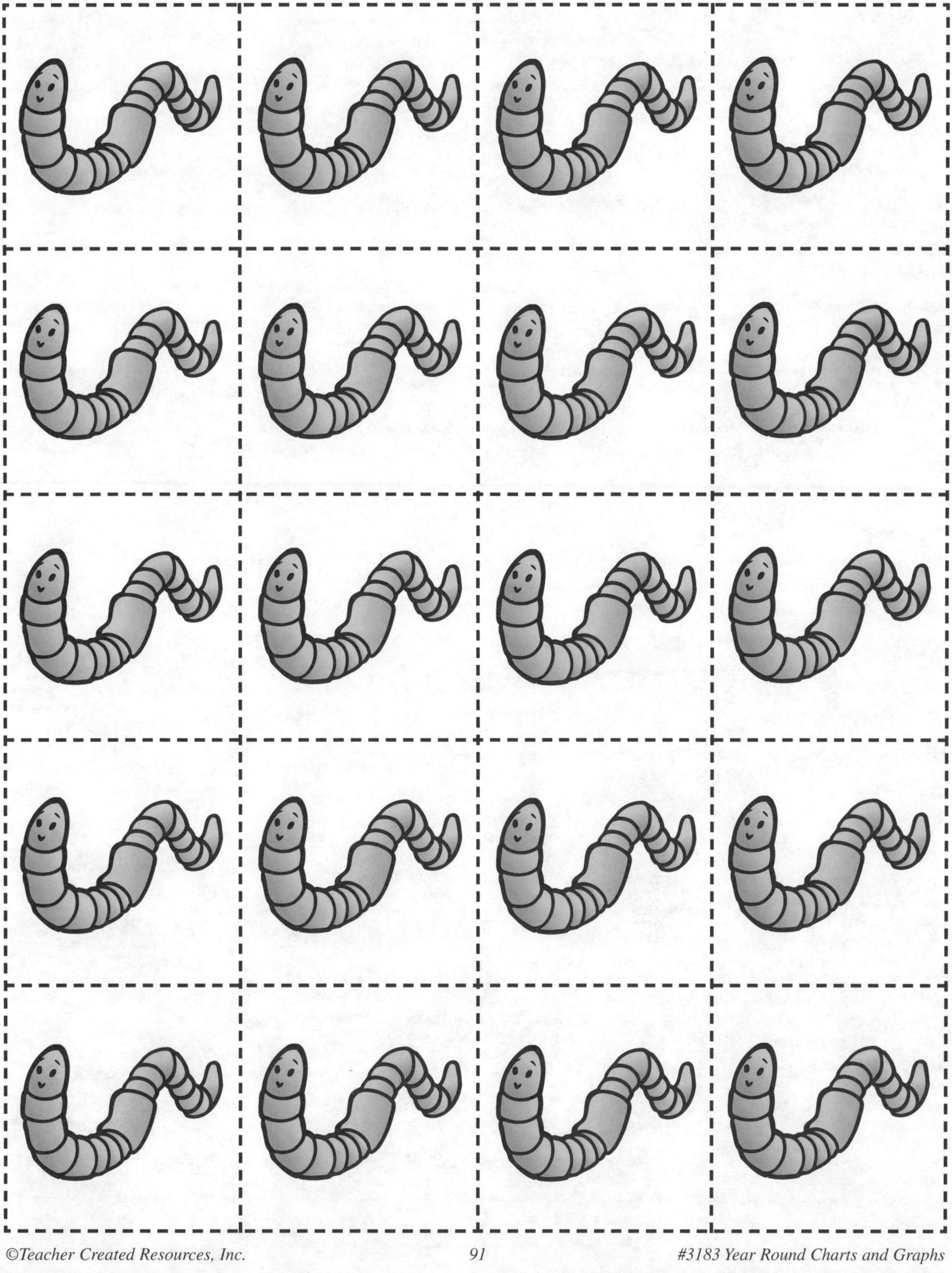

Dinosaurs

Graph Questions

Which is your favorite dinosaur?

Which dinosaur would you like to have had for a pet?

Did it eat meat or plants?

Did it walk on two or four legs?

What color do you think it was?

Do you wish dinosaurs were alive today? (Yes/No)

Tyrannosaurus

Stegosaurus

Triceratops

Pteradactyl

Apatosaurus

Yes

No

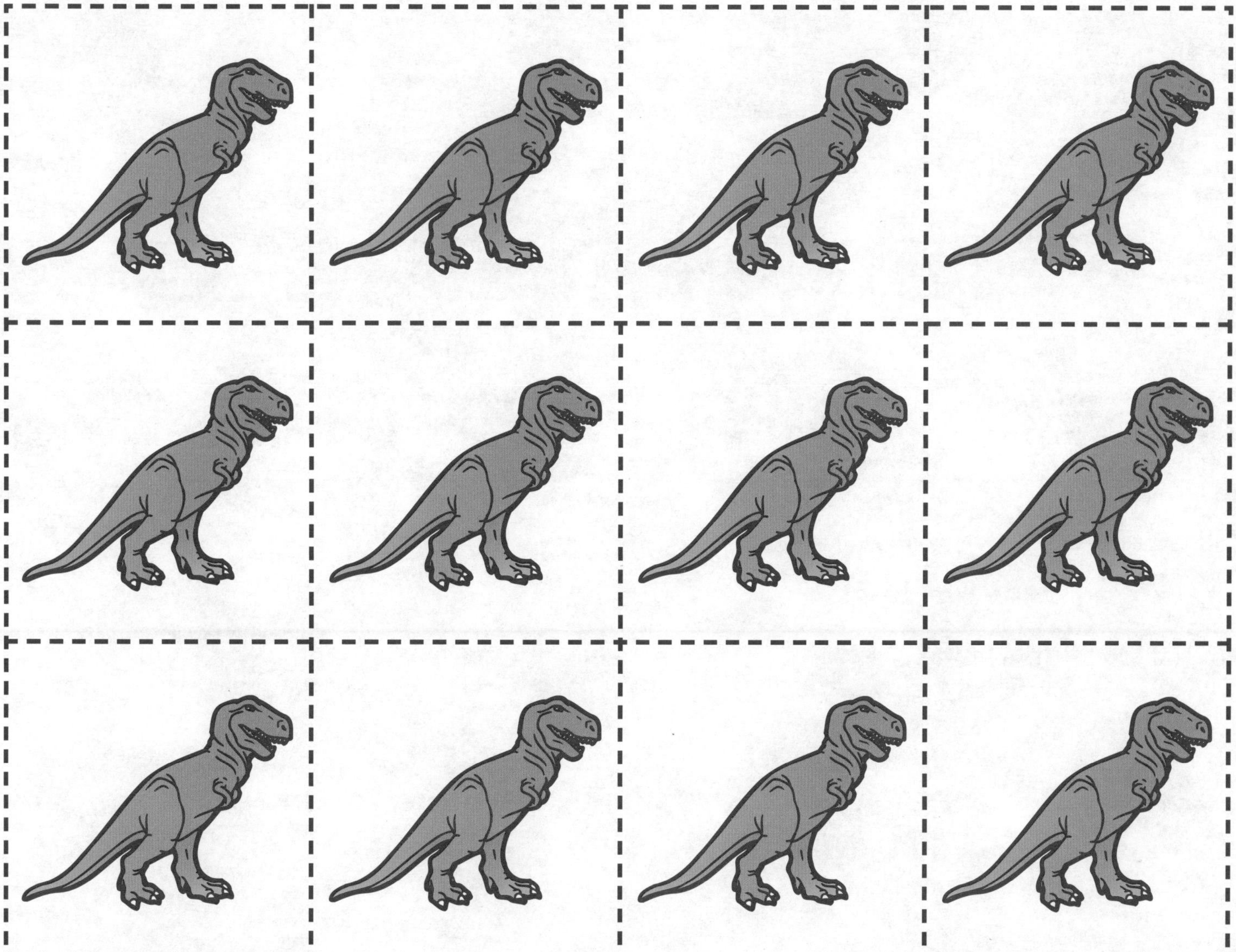

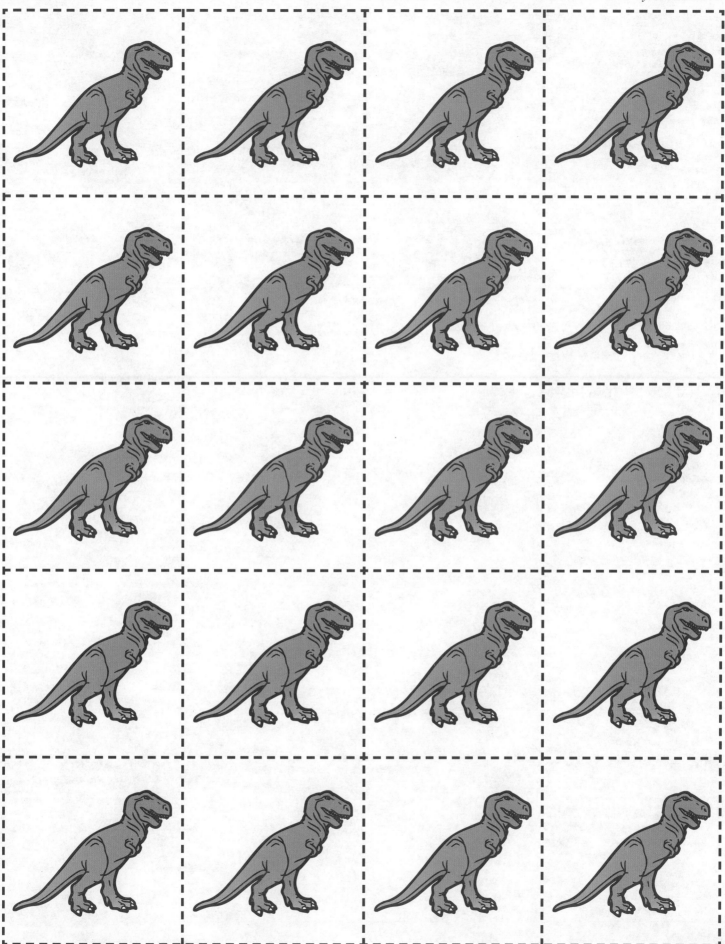

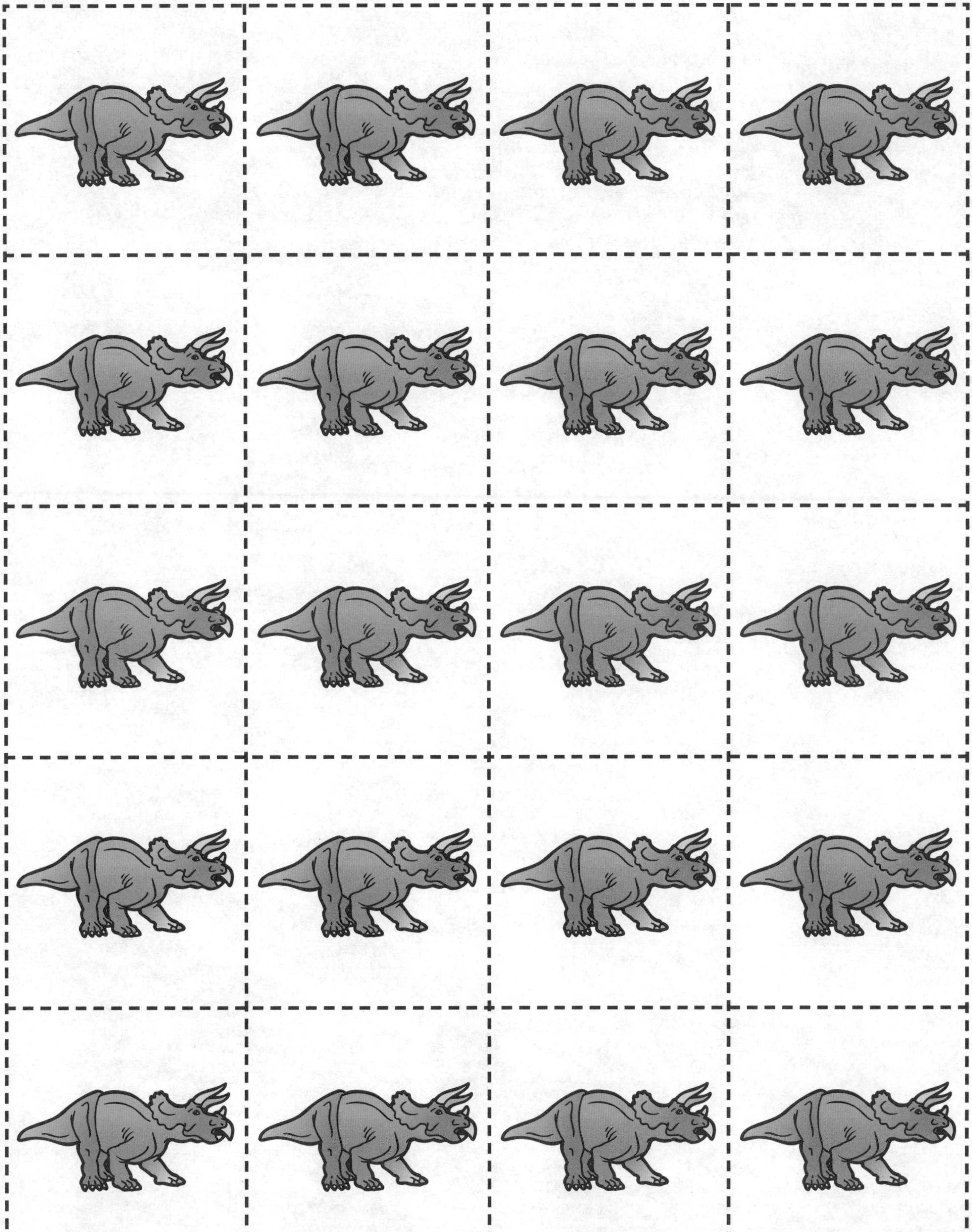

Fruit

Graph Questions

Which is your favorite fruit?

What shape is it?

What color is it?

Do you like fruit? (Yes/No)

How do you like your apples? (sliced/sauce/pie)

Does it have seeds? (Yes/No)

Can you eat the skin? (Yes/No)

Pear

Apple

Orange

Watermelon

Grapes

Yes

No

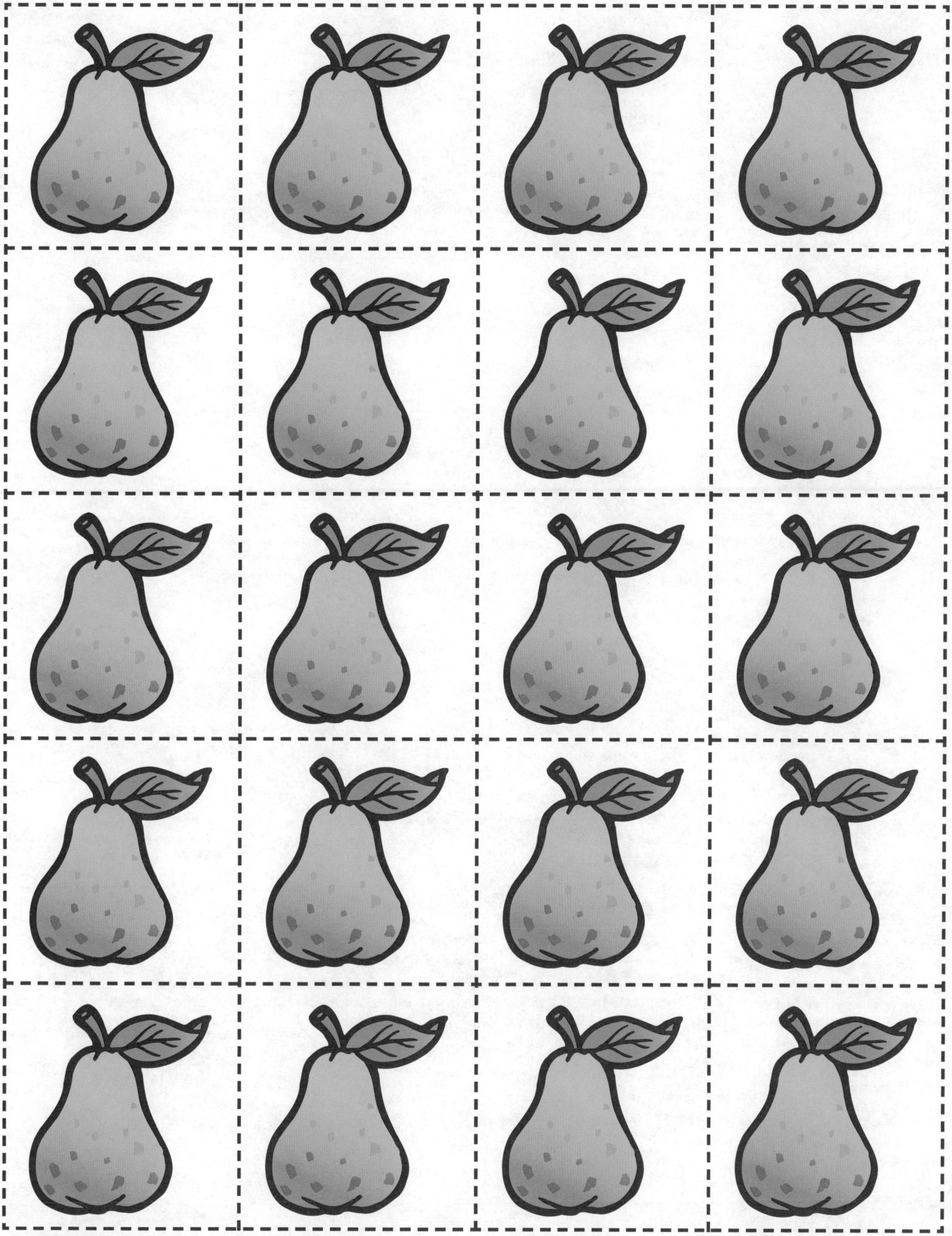

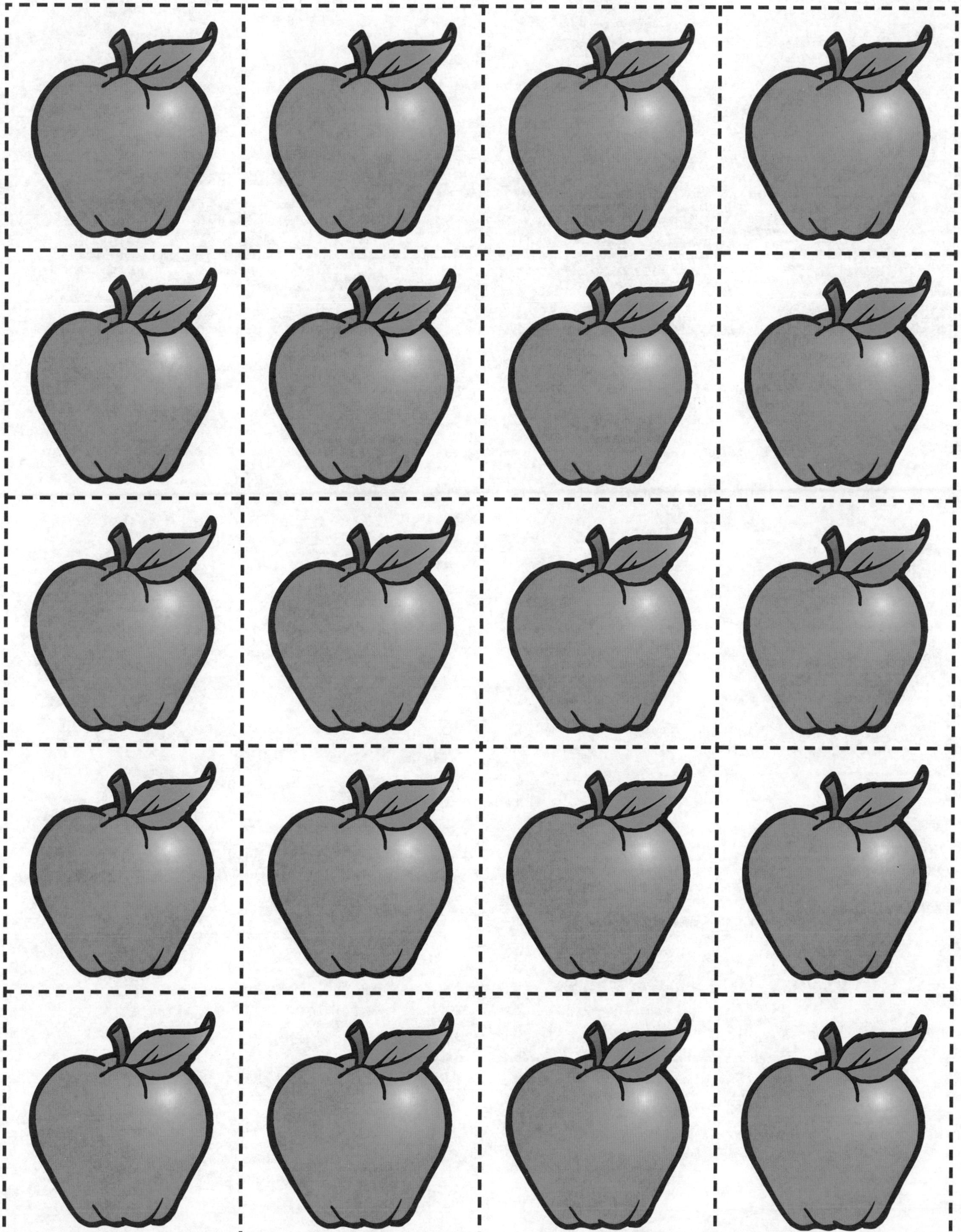

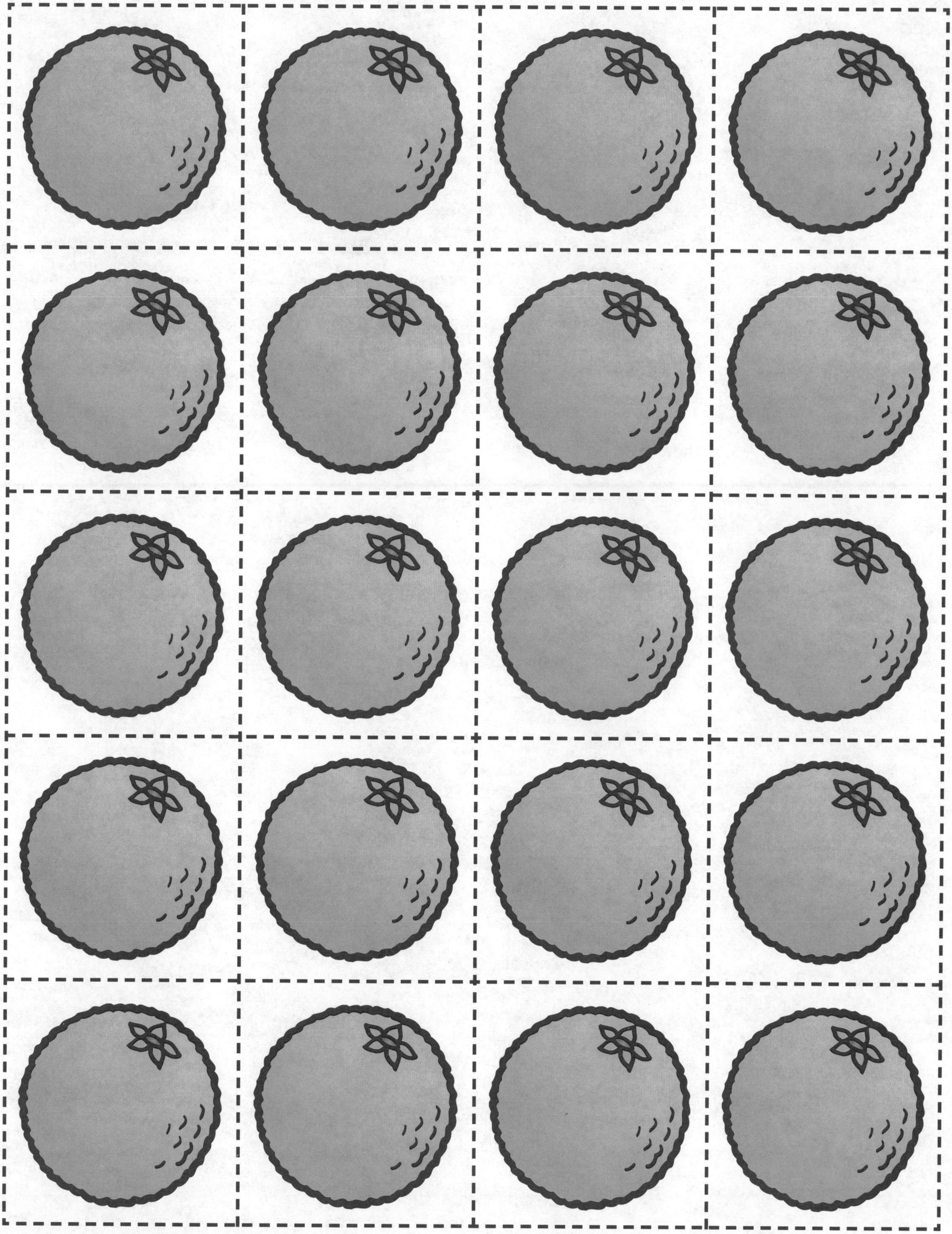

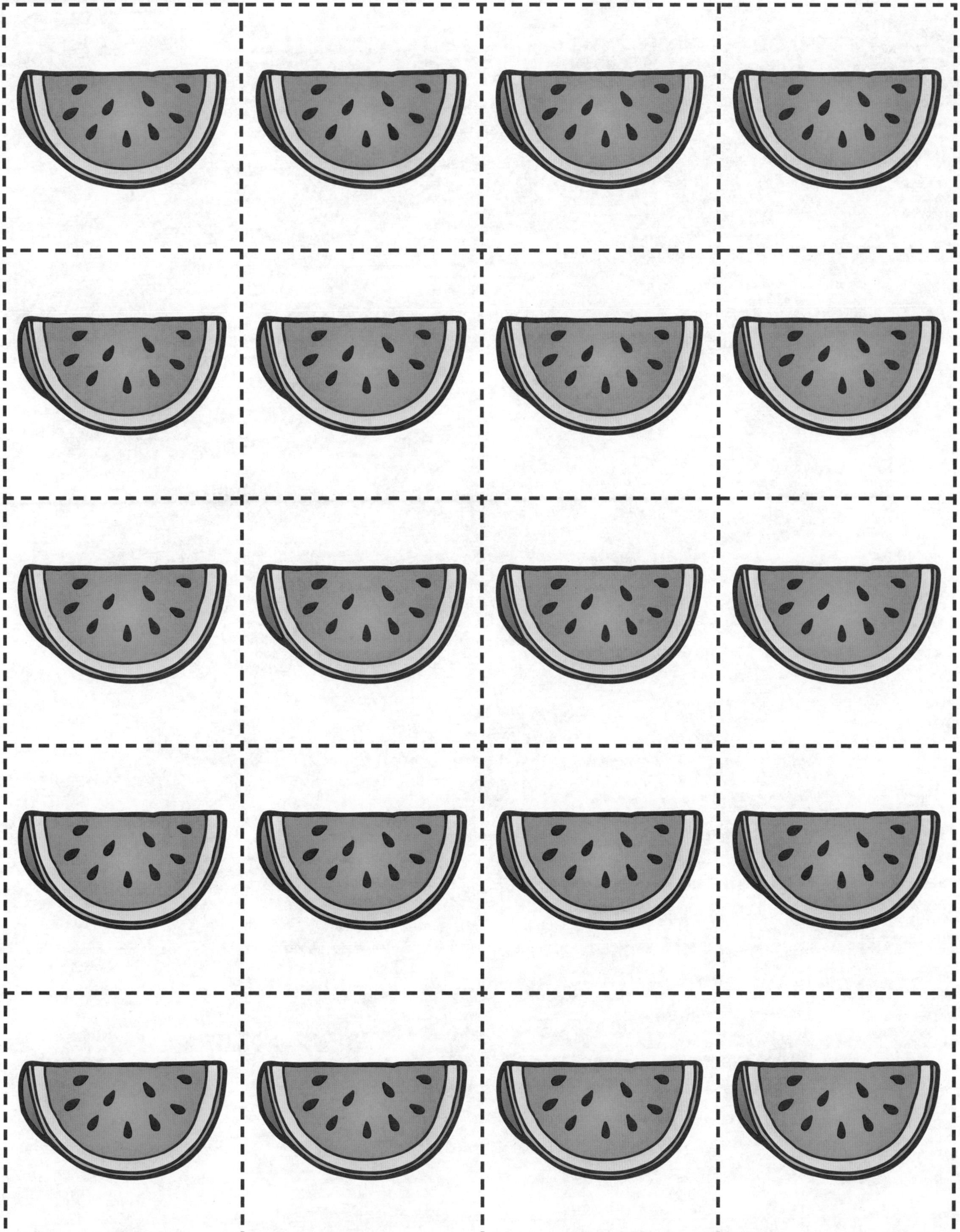

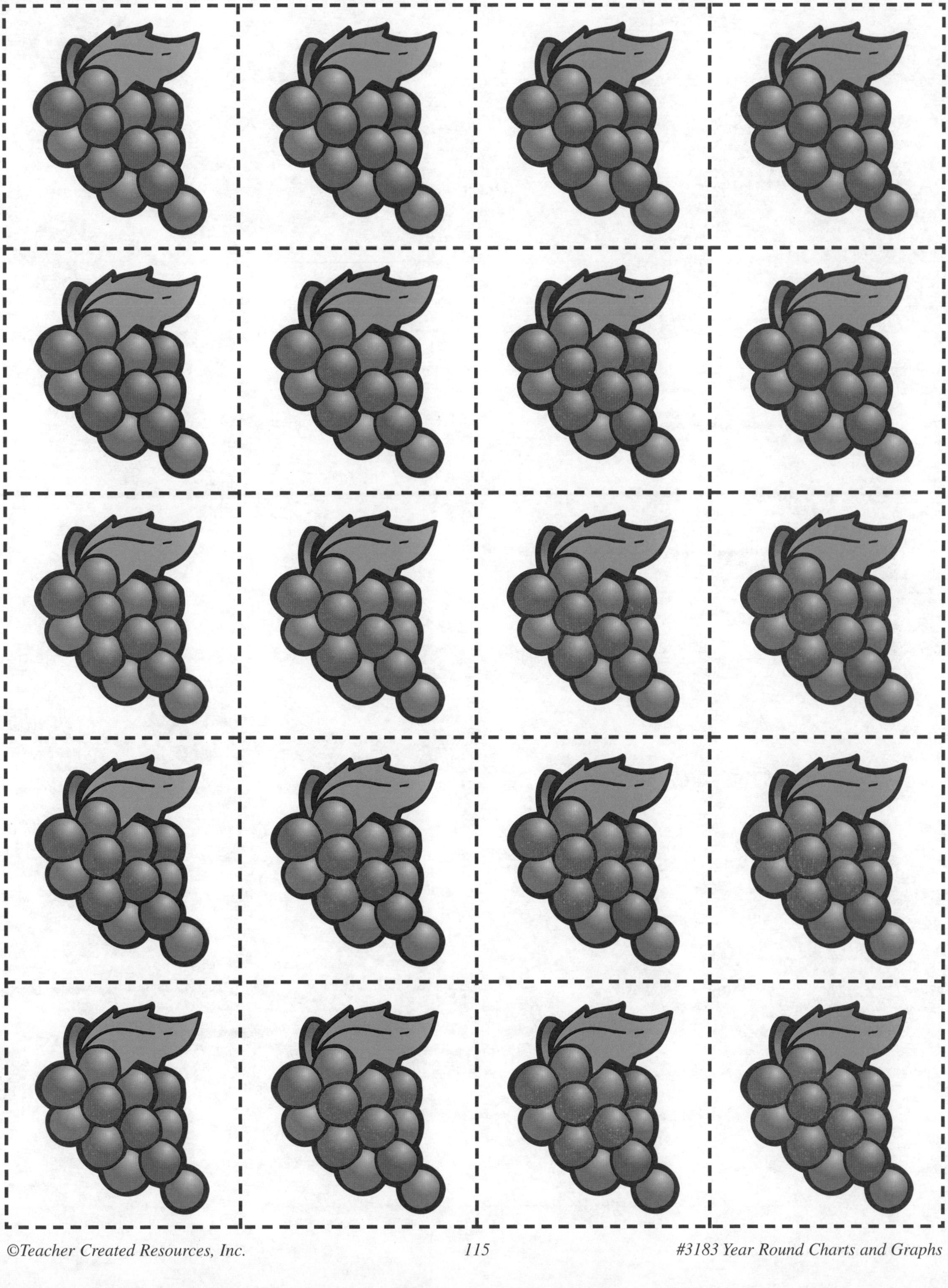

Transportation

Graph Questions

Which is your favorite type of transportation?

Does it have two wheels, four wheels, or more?

How did you get to school today?

How did you travel on your last trip?

How many people can ride in or on it?

Could it take you home by driving on the street? (Yes/No)

Car

Bus

Train

Bike

Airplane

Yes

No

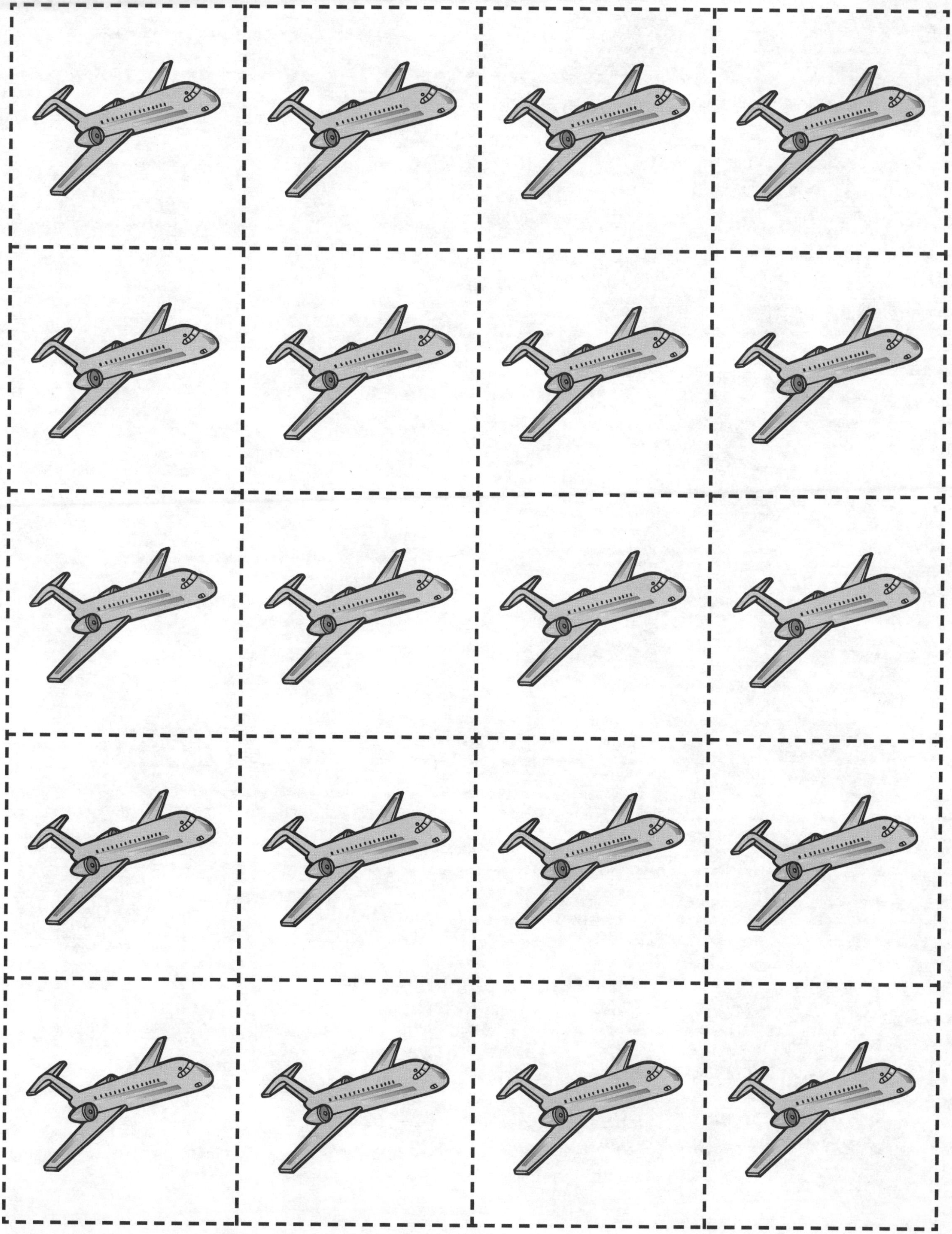

Sports

Graph Questions

Which is your favorite sport to play?

What shape is the ball?

What size is the ball?

Which ball do you play with at recess?

What do you use to play with the ball?
(hands, feet, racquet, other equipment)

Do you need equipment besides the ball to play?
(Yes/No)

Soccer

Football

Basketball

Baseball

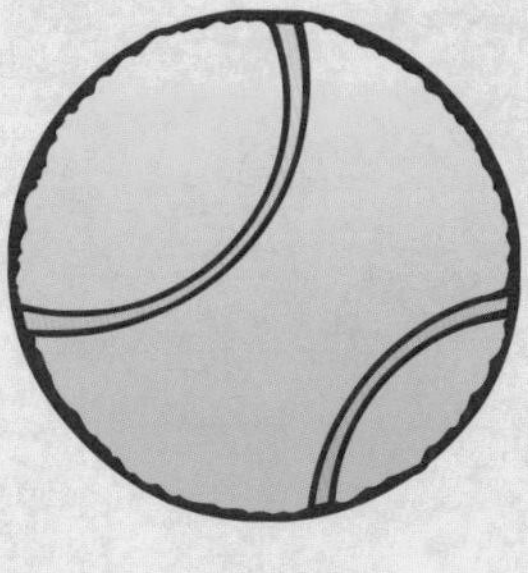

Tennis

Yes

No

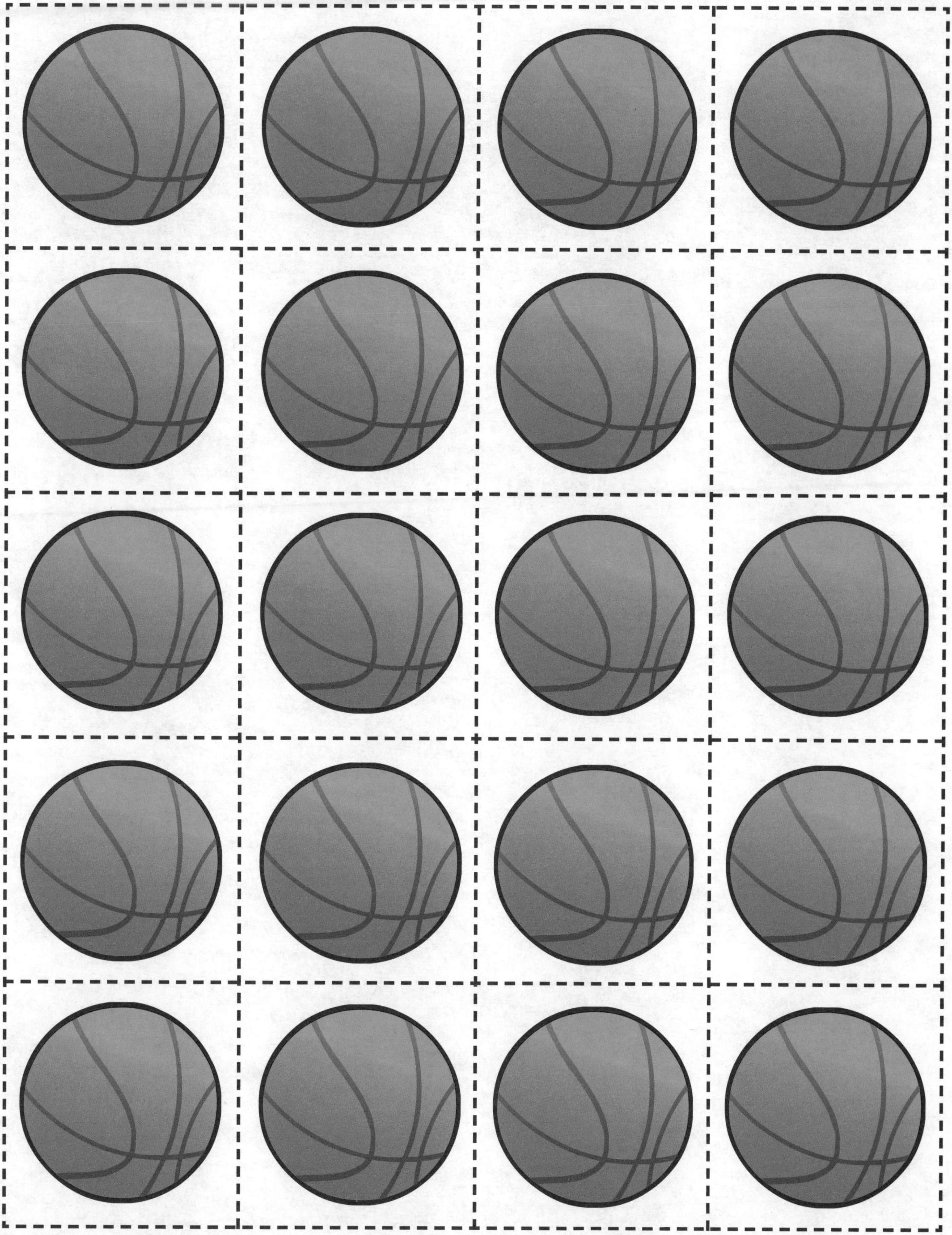

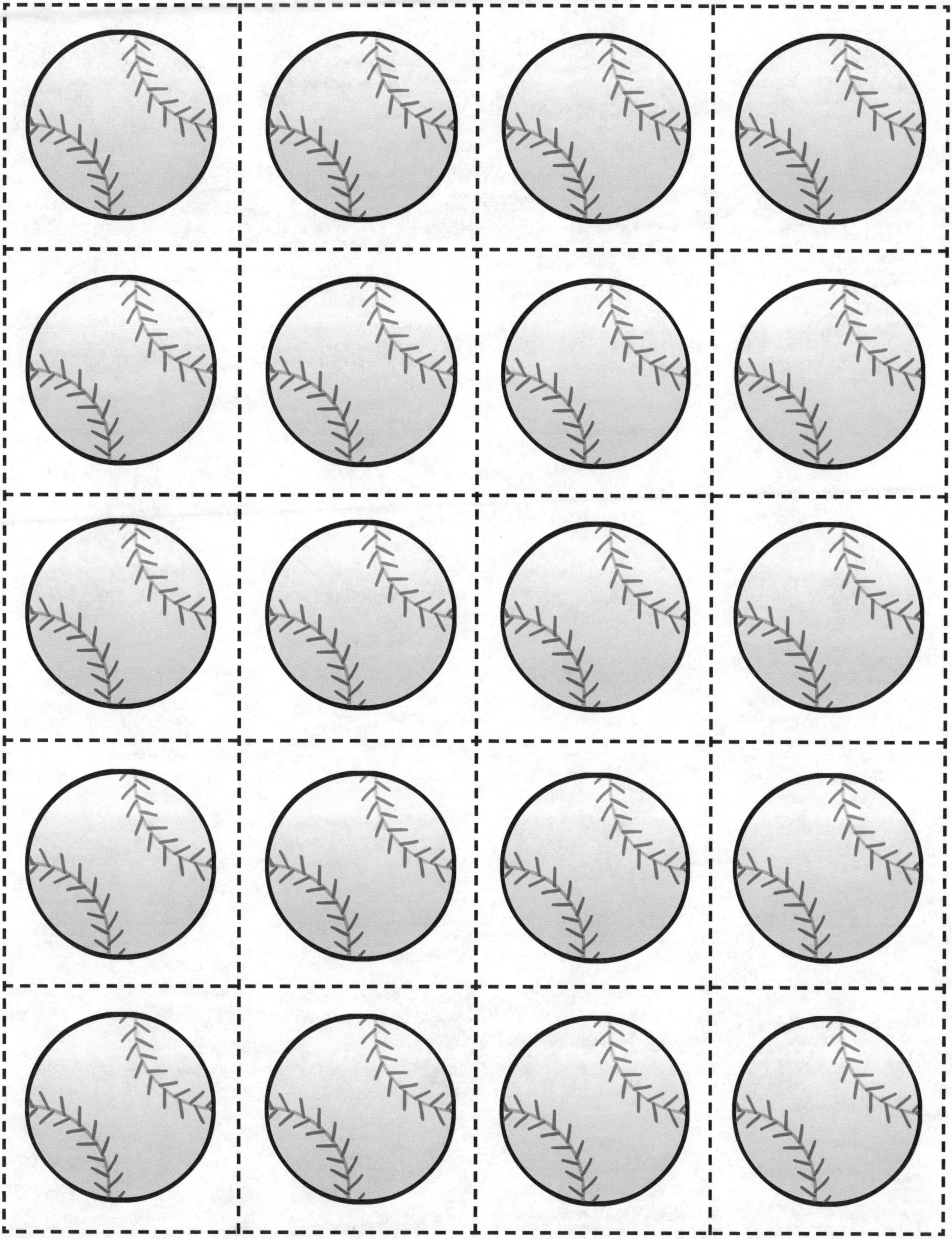

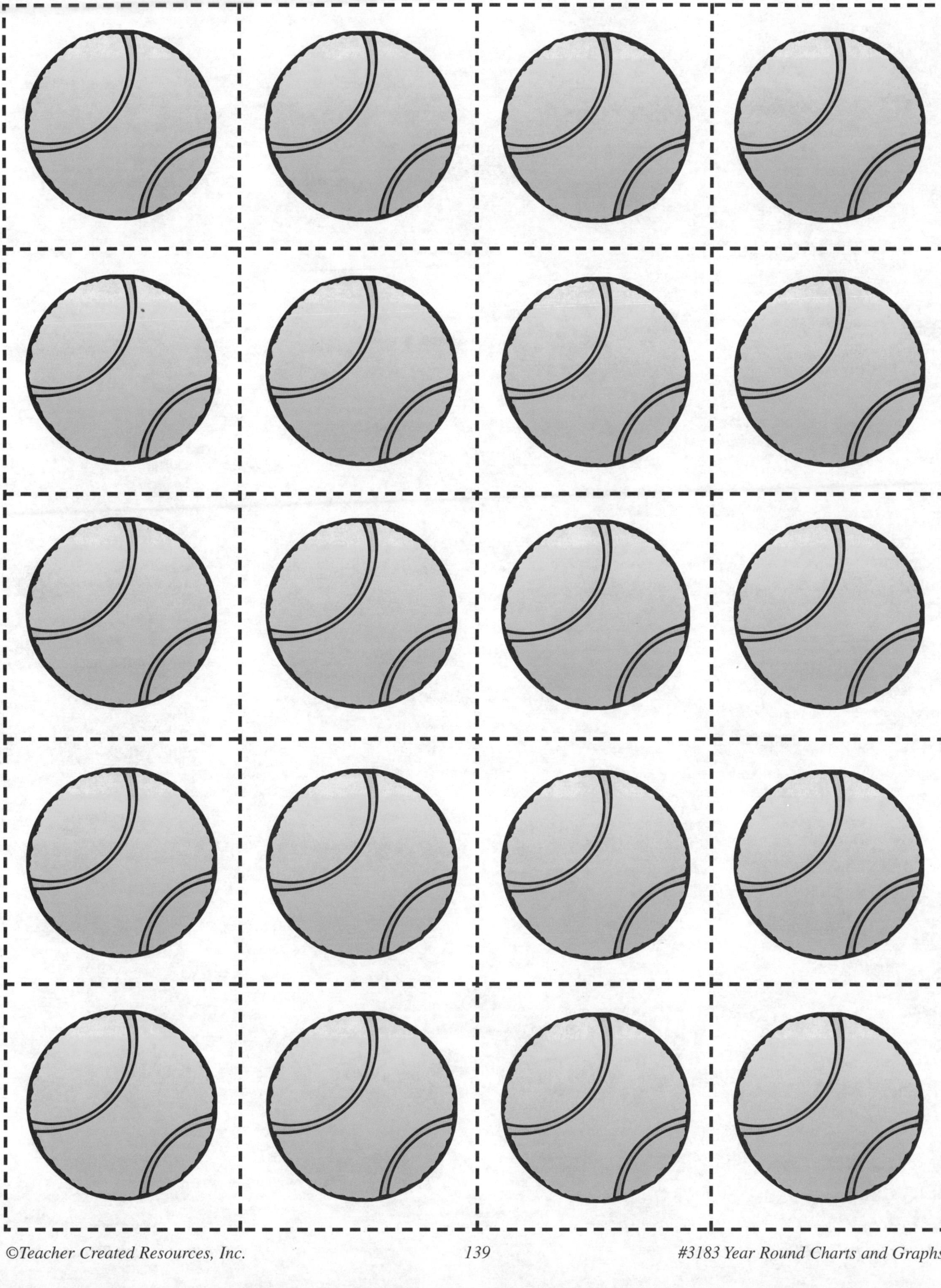

Pets

Graph Questions

Which pet do you own?

Which pet would you like to own?

Do you have a pet? (Yes/No)

Do you like dogs or cats better?

Does it have fur, feathers, or scales?

How many legs does it have?

Can you play with it? (Yes/No)

Cat

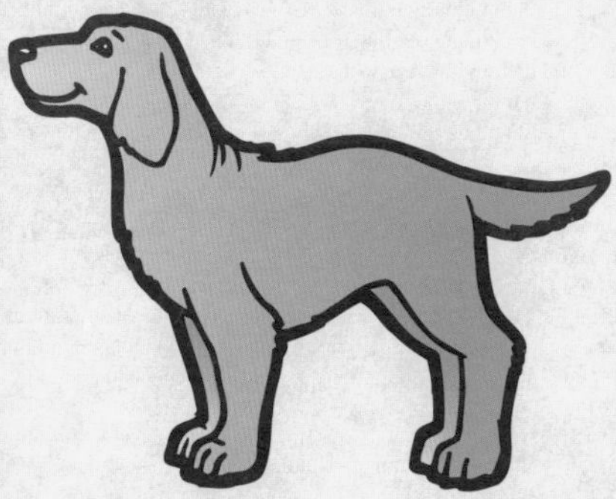

Dog

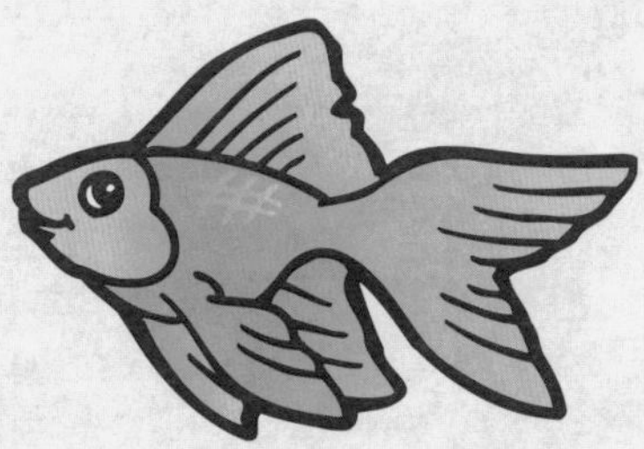

Fish

Turtle

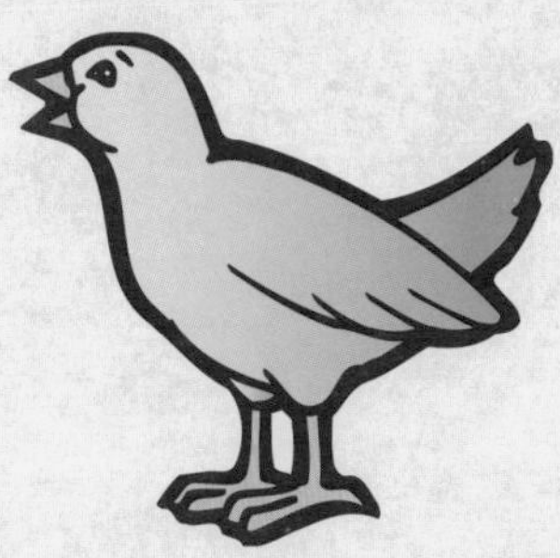

Bird

Yes

No

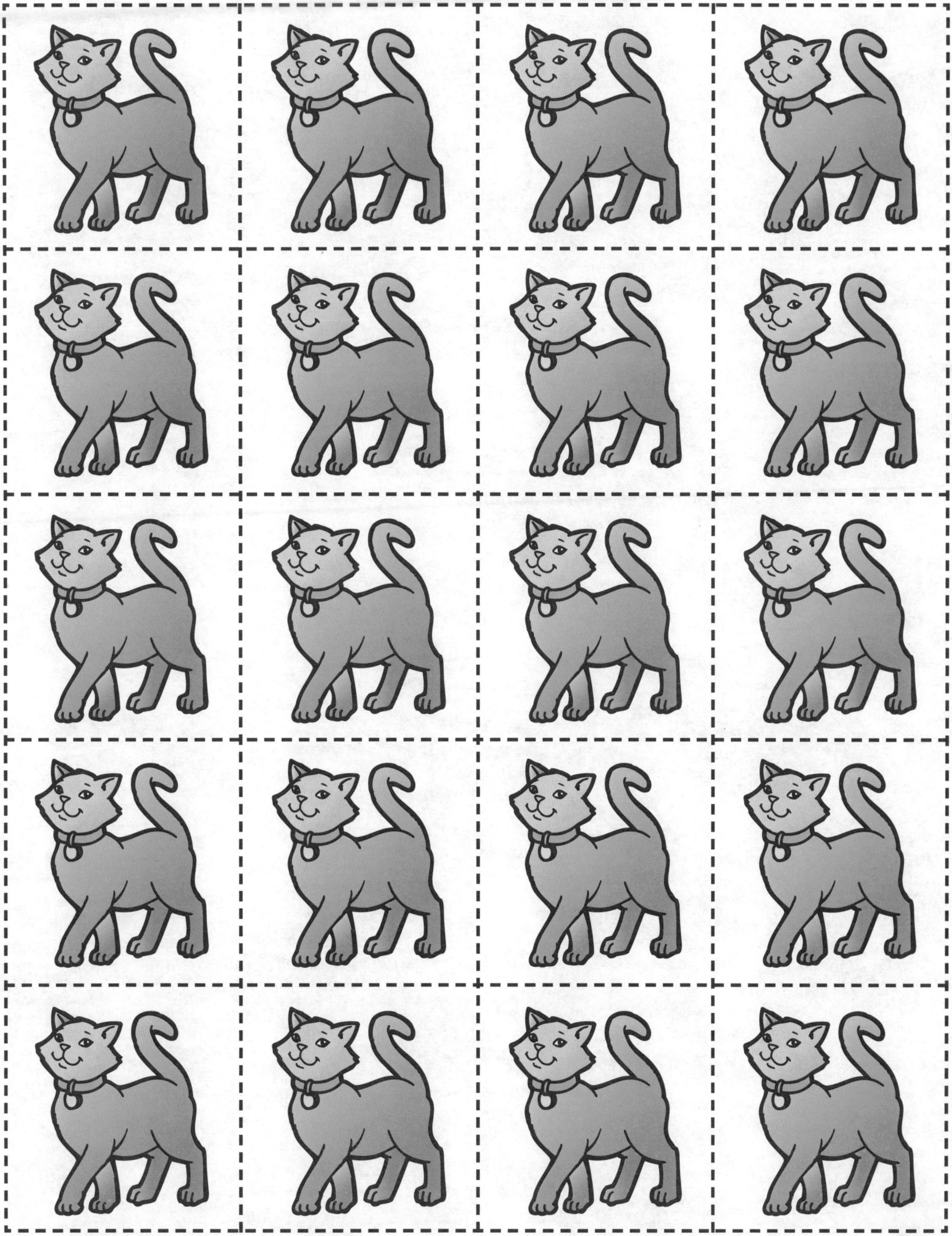

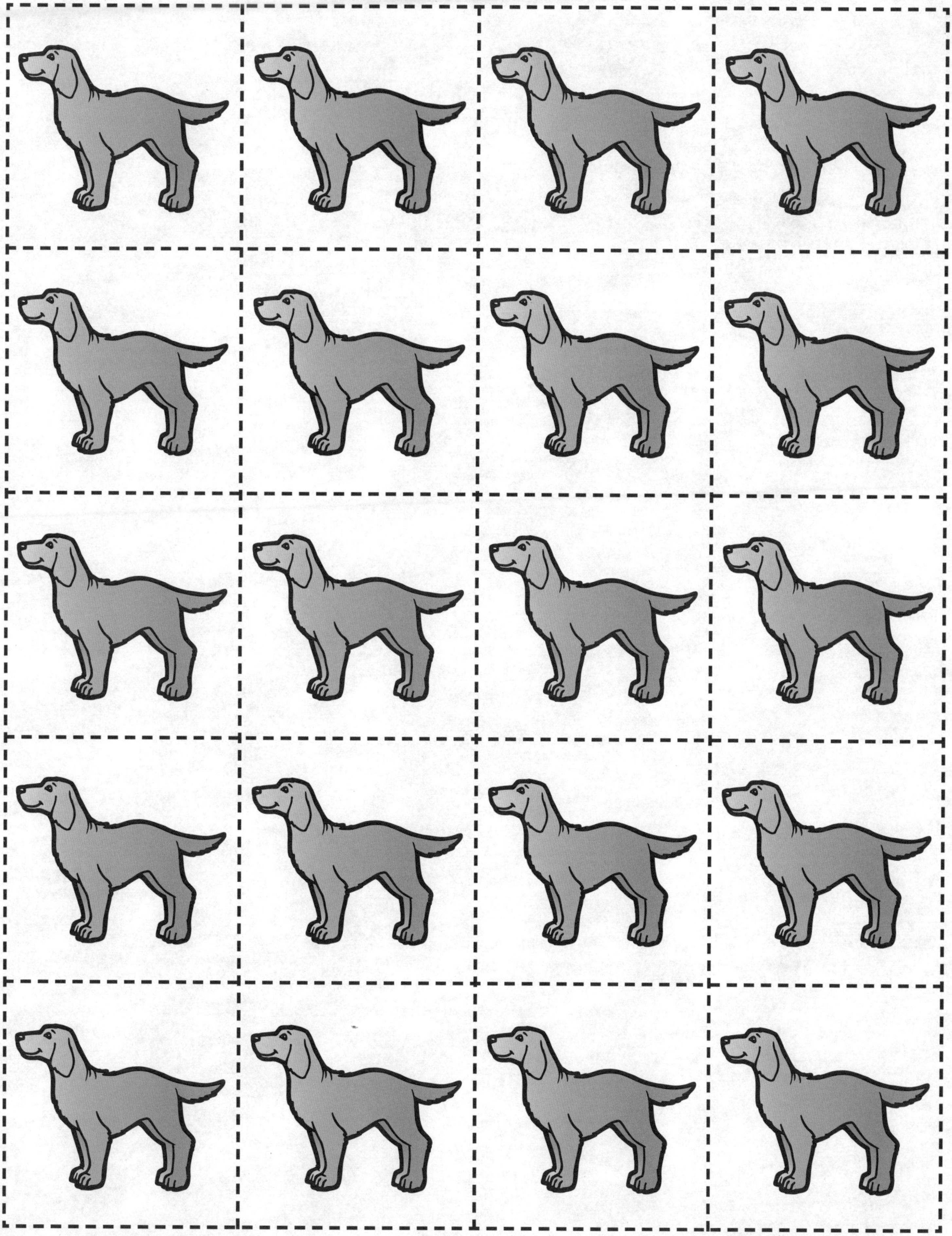

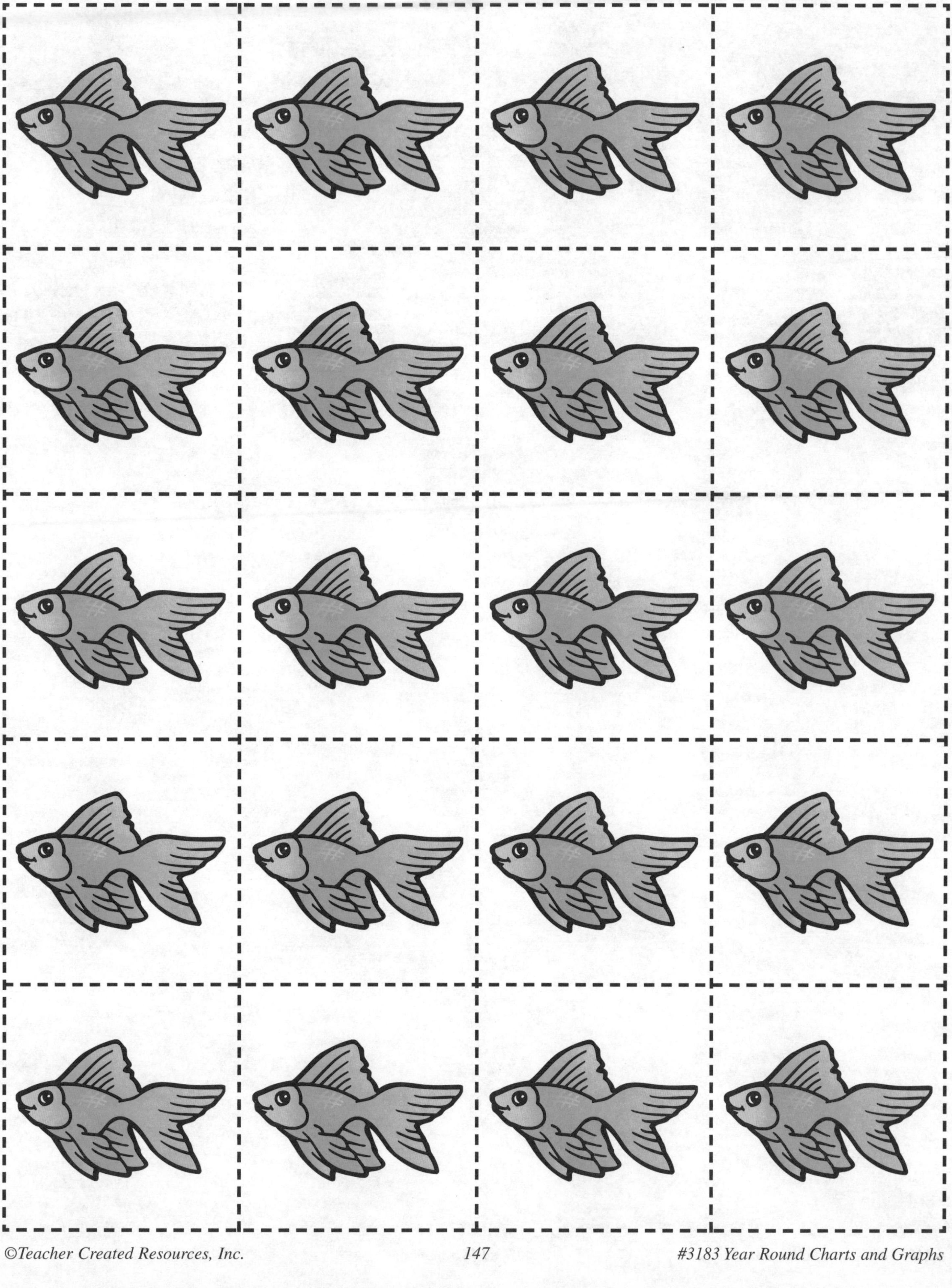

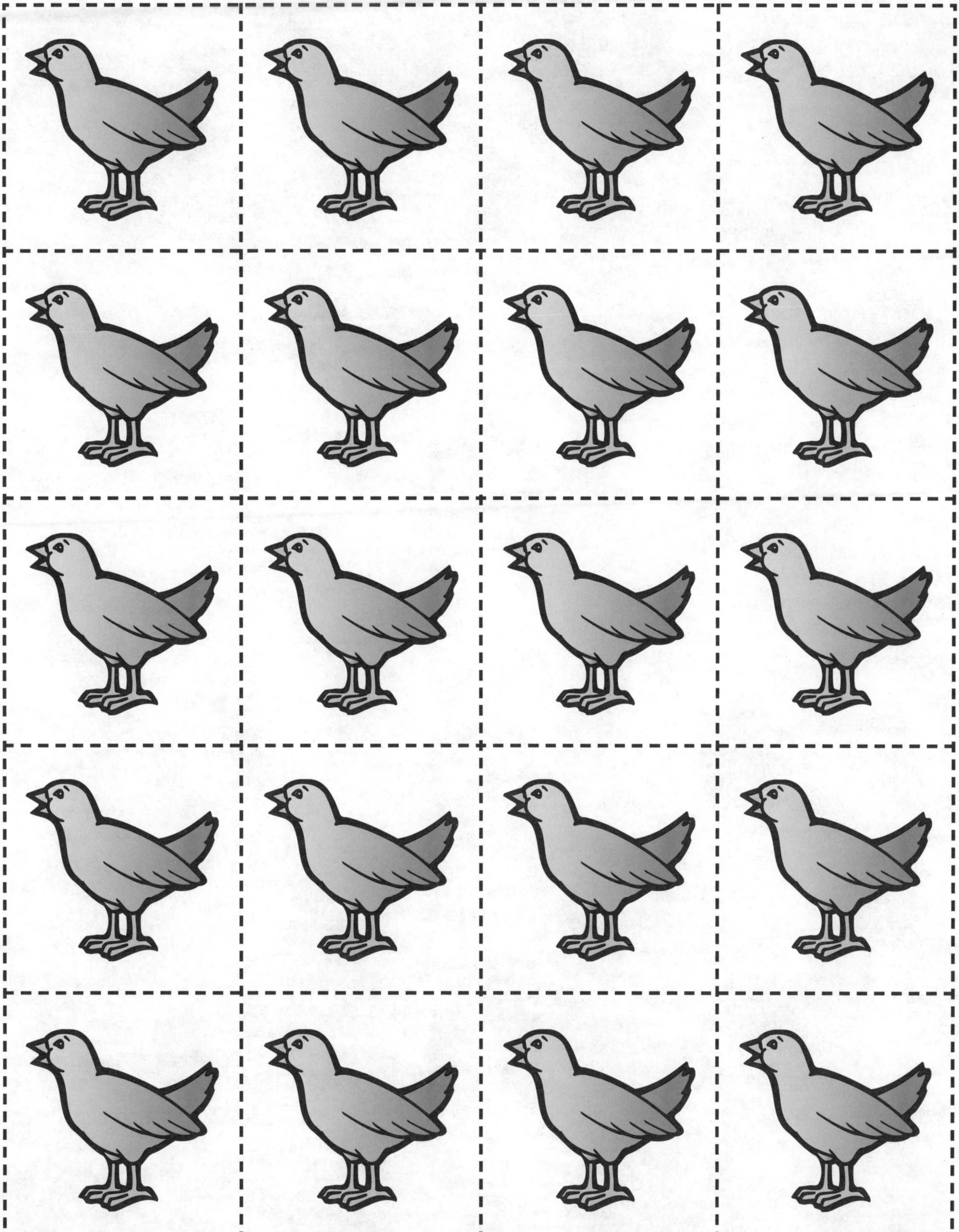

Nursery Rhymes

Graph Questions

Which is your favorite rhyme?

How many characters (people/animals) are in it?

Can you sing it? (Yes/No)

Are there animals in it? (Yes/No)

Hey Diddle Diddle

Humpty Dumpty

Jack and Jill

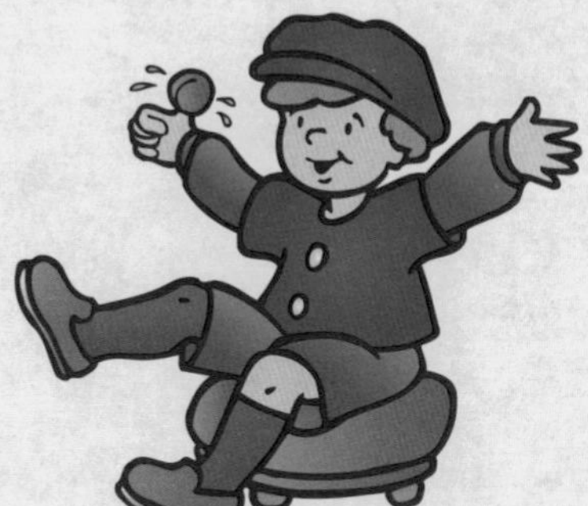

Little Jack Horner

Hickory Dickory Dock

Yes

No

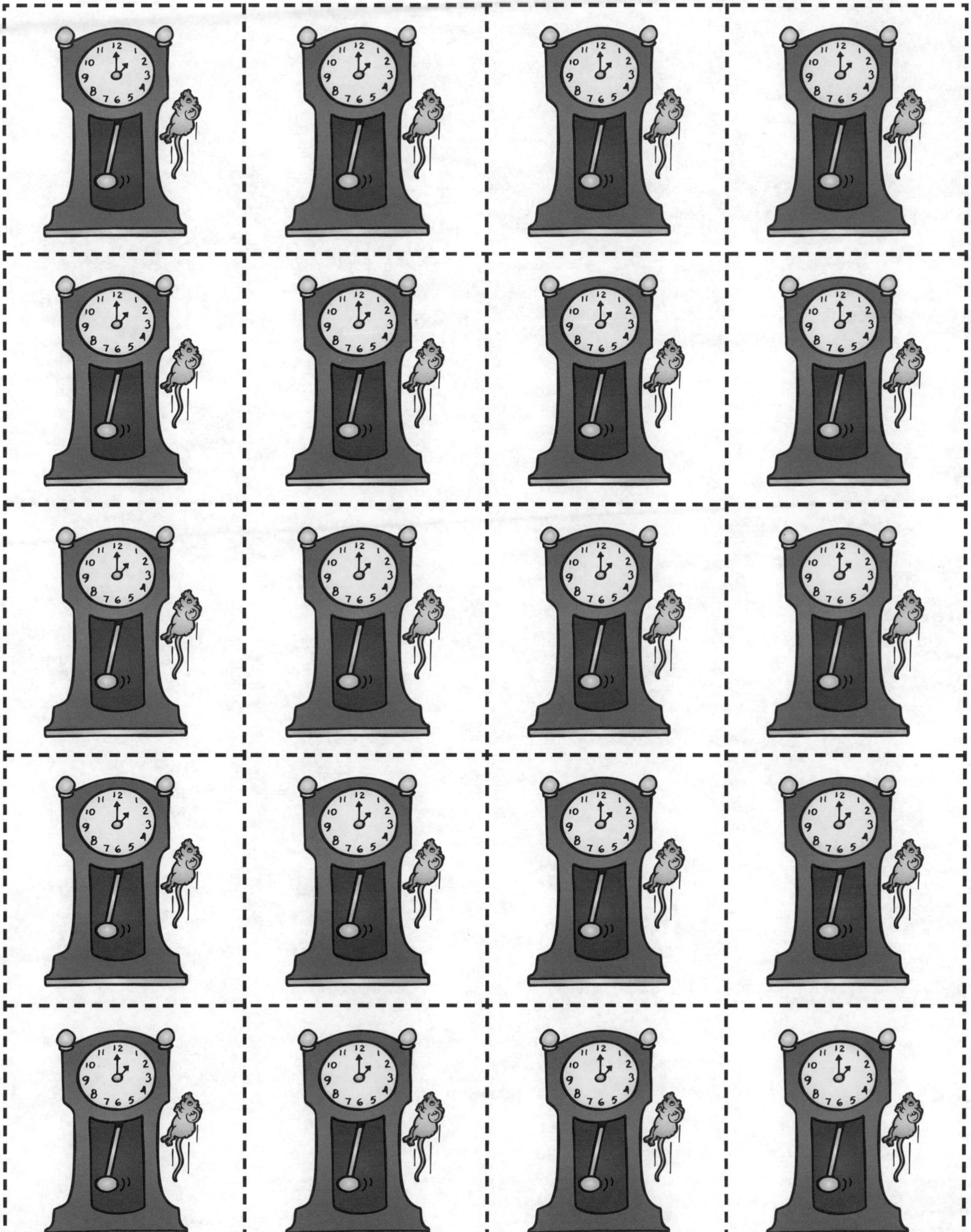

The Five Senses

Graph Questions

Which sense do you think you use most?

Which sense would you use first to learn about an apple?

What color are your eyes? (blue, brown, hazel, green)

Are you right-handed or left-handed?

Touch

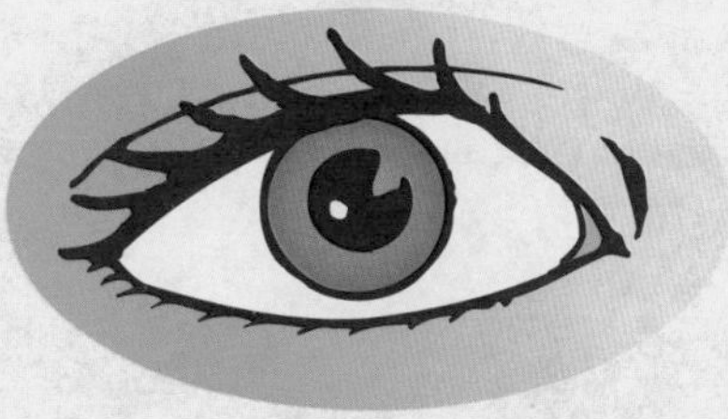

Sight

Hearing

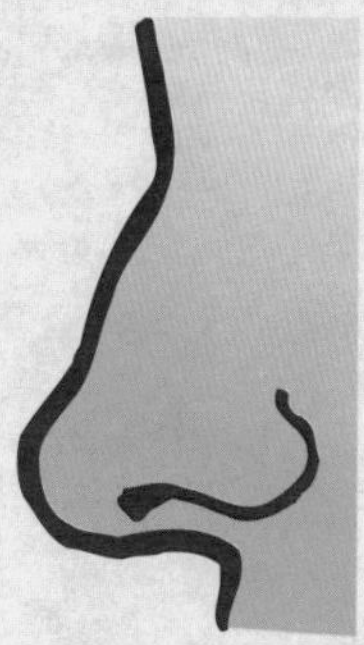

Smell

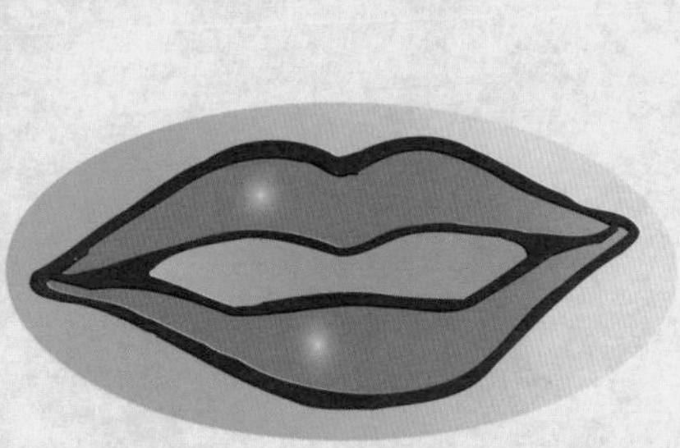

Taste

Yes

No

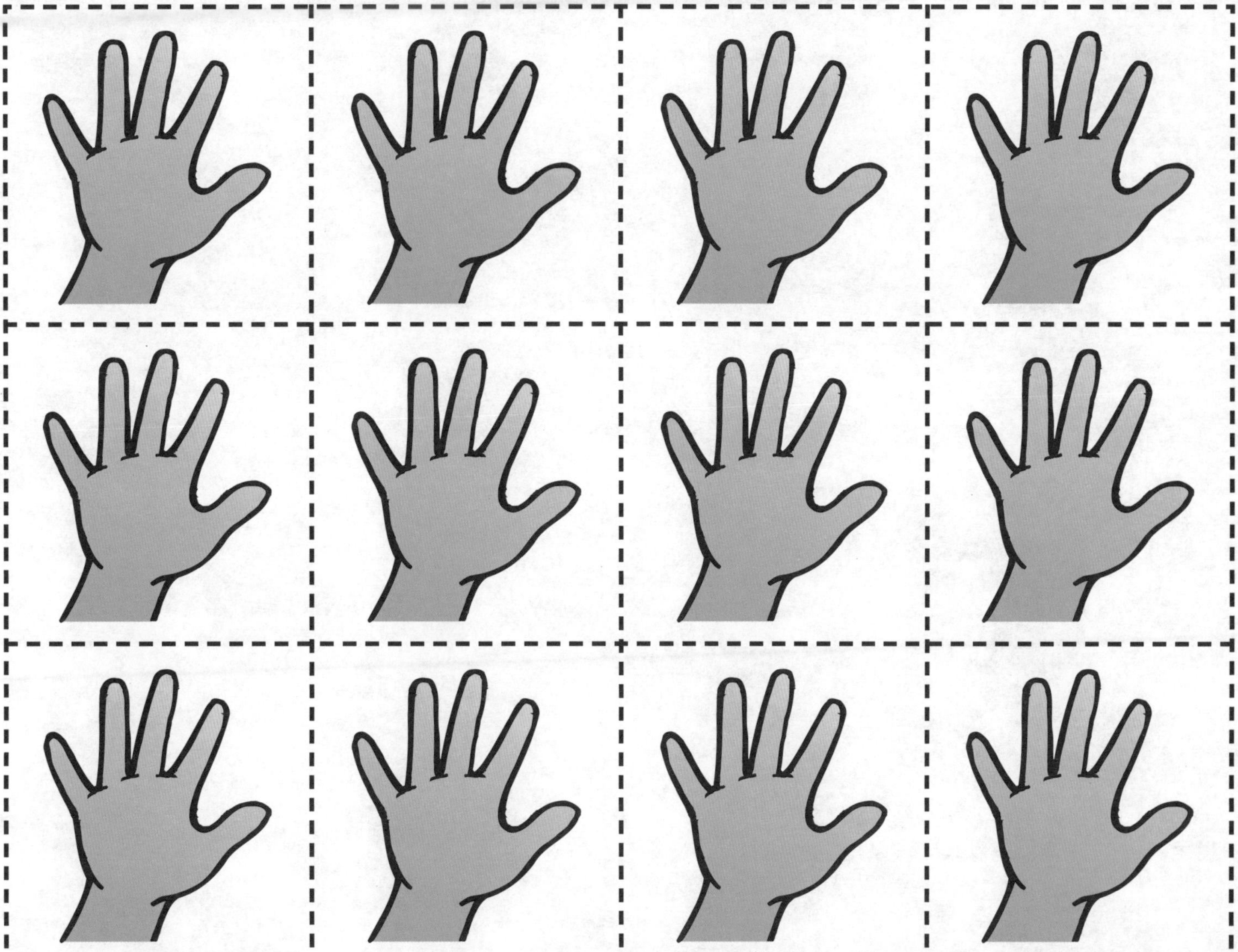

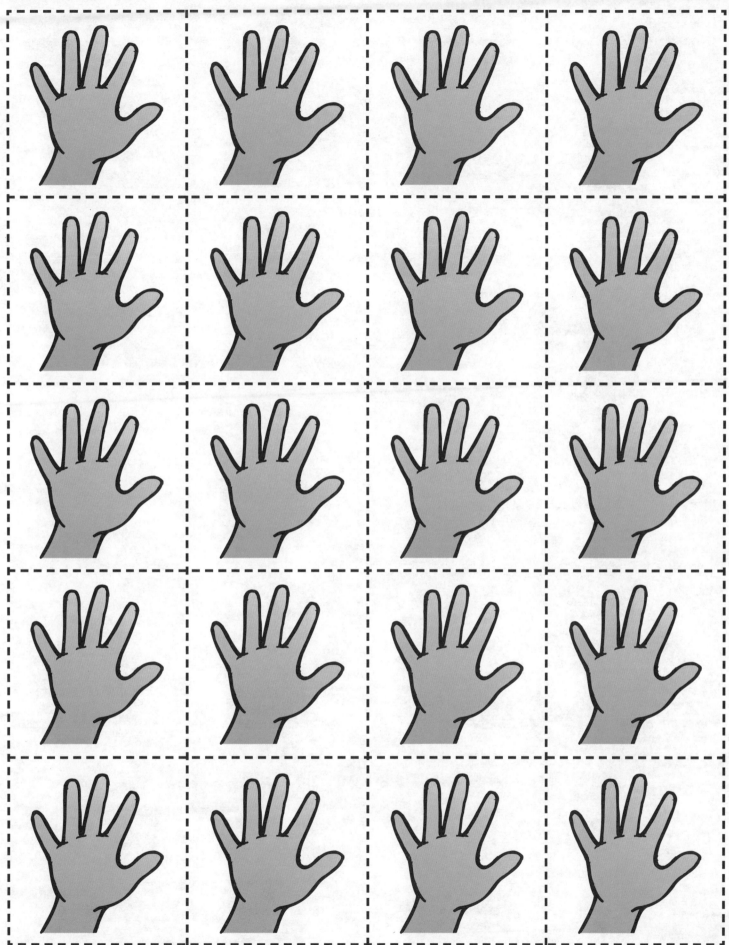

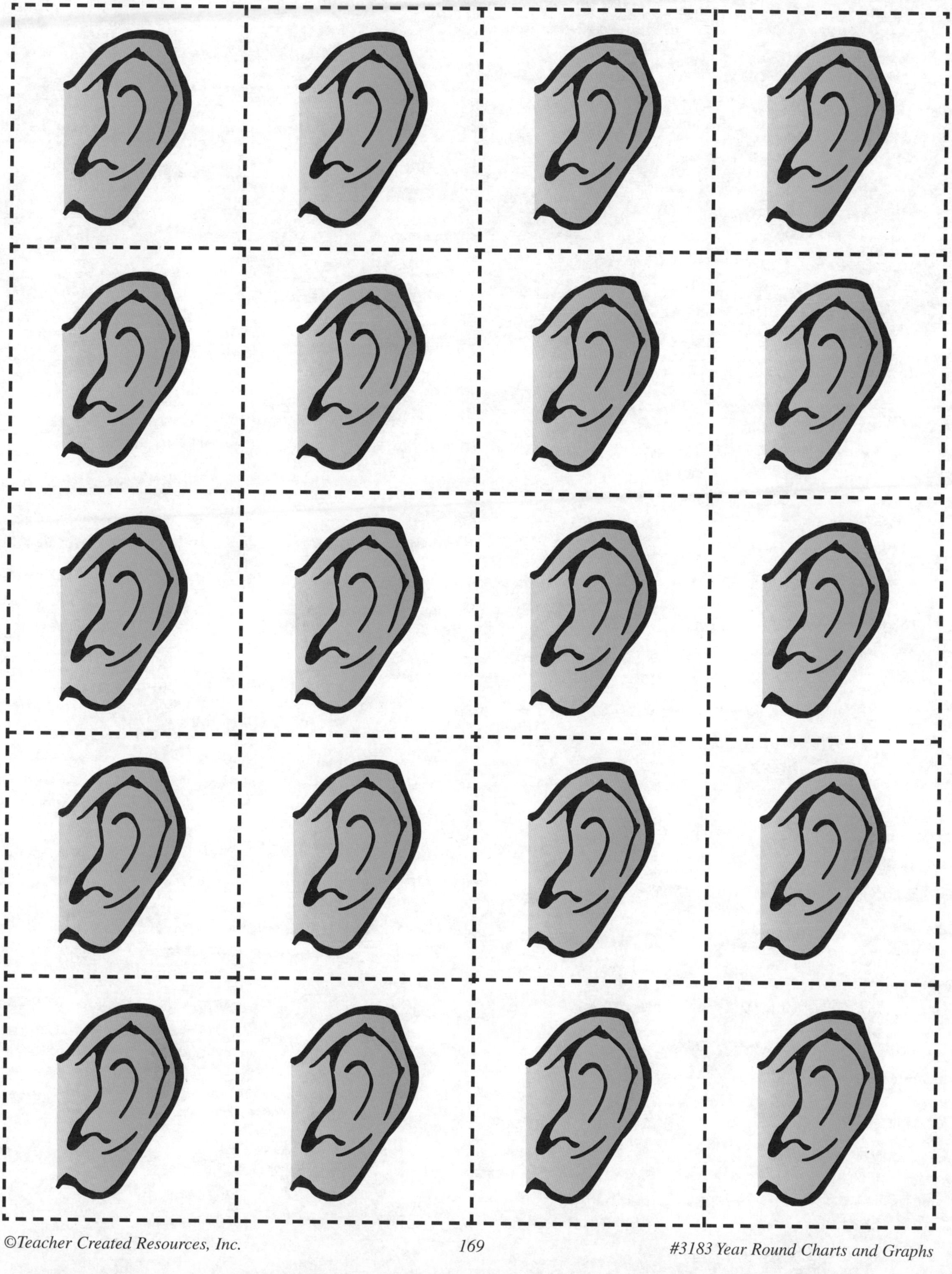

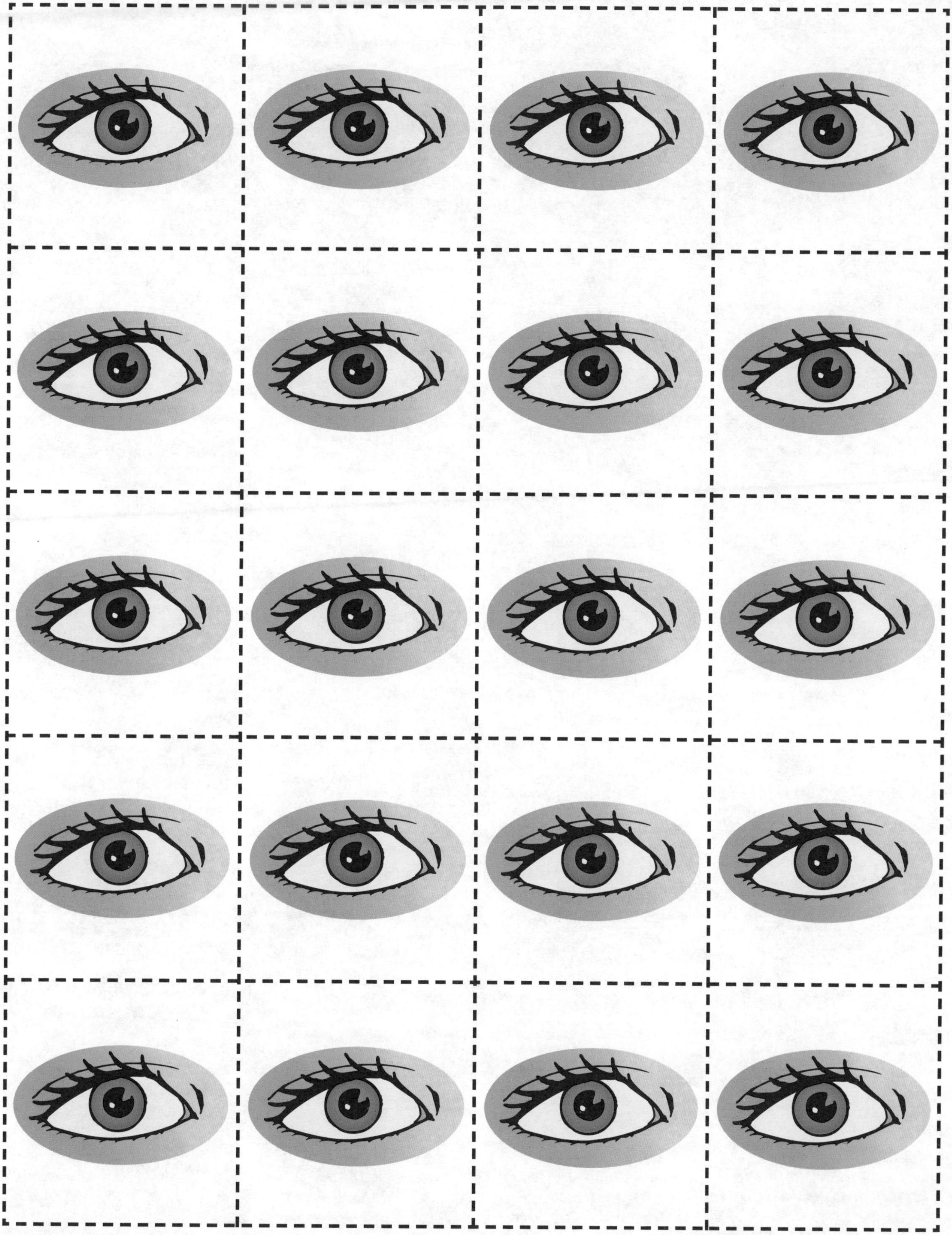

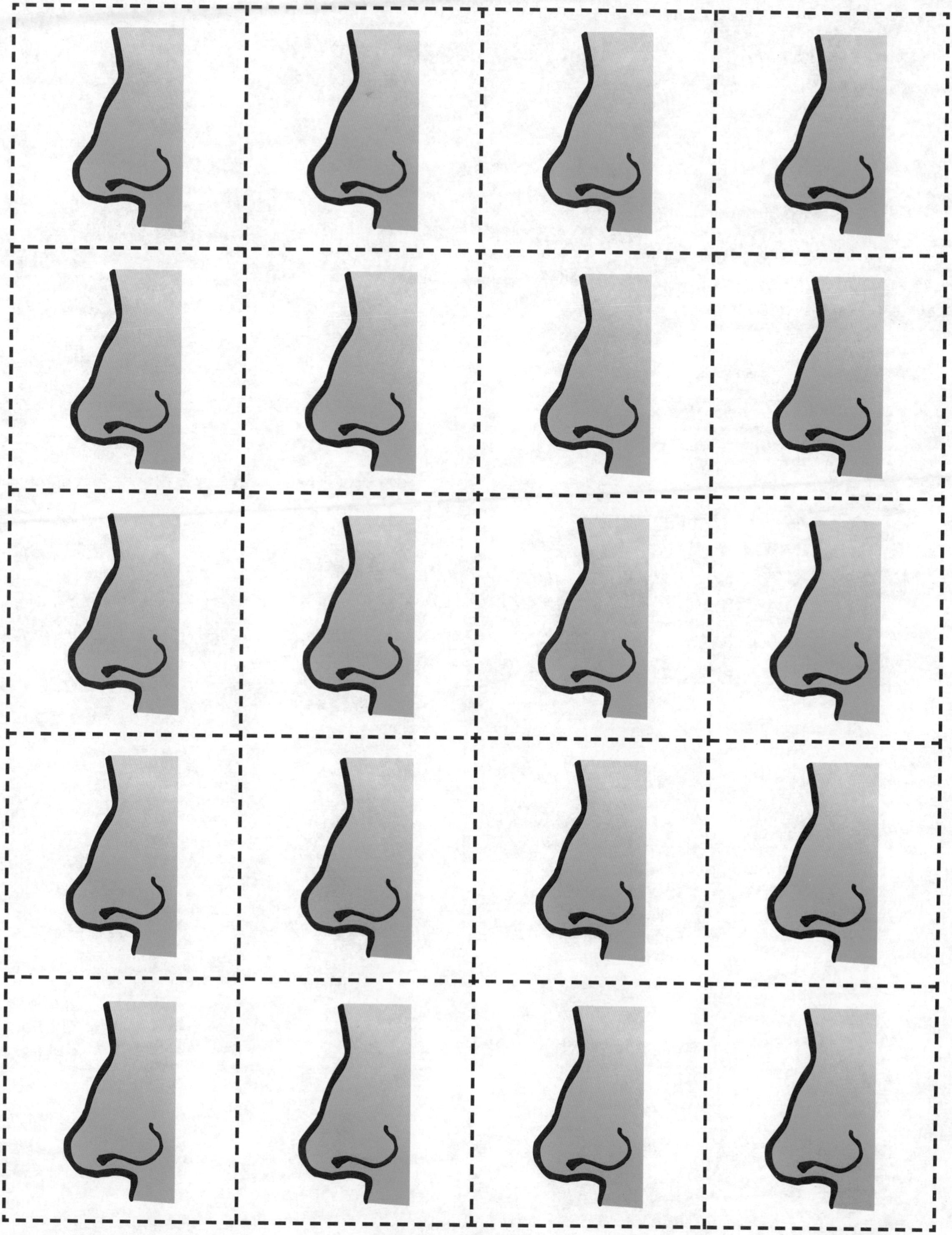